POINT MAN

TAKING NEW GROUND

STEVE FARRAR

WITH DAVE BRANON

MULTNOMAH BOOKS · SISTERS, OREGON

POINT MAN DEVOTIONAL
published by Multnomah Books
a part of the Questar publishing family

© 1996 by Steve Farrar
International Standard Book Number: 0-88070-825-5

Cover design by David Uttley
Cover illustration by Greg Tess

Printed in the United States of America

Most Scripture quotations are from: *New American Standard Bible* (NASB)
© 1960, 1977 by the Lockman Foundation

Also quoted:

The Holy Bible, New International Version (NIV)
© 1973, 1984 by International Bible Society, used by permission of Zondervan Publishing House

The Living Bible (TLB) © 1971 by Tyndale House Publishers

For information:
Questar Publishers, Inc.
Post Office Box 1720
Sisters, Oregon 97759

96 97 98 99 00 01 02 — 10 9 8 7 6 5 4 3 2 1

CONTENTS

FOREWORD

Any NFL or college football coach will tell you the same thing. The quality of play that goes on before a packed stadium is determined by the quality of daily practices that take place with just a handful of people looking on.

The same thing is true in the Christian life. Stay with me for a few pages and I'll explain how this book and your ability to lead your family fits into that concept.

Last week I flew into Atlanta to meet with about fifteen men — men in various positions of group leadership from around the country. When the shuttle bus pulled up in front of the hotel, I realized that I had been there before. Almost six years ago to the day, I had spoken at a college conference in the same airport hotel. Why had I remembered it so clearly? This was the place where I had finished the manuscript of my first book, *Point Man*. I can still remember taking time between talks to feverishly finish the final chapter and get it off to the publisher via Fed Ex.

I had never written a book before. And there were frequent times while writing when I'd hit the wall and get stuck. In order to four-wheel drive myself out of those "stuck" periods, I did two things. As I sat, staring at the screen of my Mac, the first thing I did was to ask myself a question. Who am I trying to reach? The answer was very clear and very simple. I was trying to reach men. Specifically, Christian men. And any other man who loved his family and wanted to get serious about leading his family.

That, in itself, was unique...writing a book to men! Back in 1989, publishers didn't publish books to men. That's because there wasn't a Christian men's movement in 1989. Guys weren't filling stadiums by the thousands in 1989. Back then you'd be lucky to get 50 guys to show up for a church men's retreat. In other words, nothing real big in terms of numbers was happening with Christian men. That's why any publisher worth his salt would tell you that books to men didn't sell because "Christian men didn't read books." But in my gut, I didn't buy that. I wanted to go after those guys and write a book that would equip them rather than bore them.

The second thing I did when I hit the wall was a little strange. In order to pump myself up, I prayed and asked God to do something absurdly extreme. I asked God to let me reach 100,000 men through this book. That was a huge prayer in 1989. Not only did Christian publishers not publish books to Christian men, but Christian men didn't go into Christian bookstores. It would have been a stretch to ask that 10,000 men would read it. But I was asking for 100,000.

In order to help me understand what reaching 100,000 men would actually look like, I simply remembered attending the 1966 Rose Bowl in Pasadena that pitted Michigan State against UCLA. There were over 100,000 screaming fans in that stadium, and along with my dad and my brothers, I was right in the middle of them.

It dawned on me one day as I was writing that if someone were to call me and say, "Hey, Steve, we've got a football stadium full of 100,000 guys who want to follow Christ and be committed husbands and fathers. Would you come and talk to these guys?"

Of course, in 1989 the idea of filling a football stadium with a bunch of guys for that purpose was not even in the realm of possibility. It was such an outlandish idea that I never mentioned it to anyone nor did I for a moment ever consider the possibility that it could happen. In my mind, since I would never have the opportunity to speak to a stadium full of men, the next best thing would be for God to somehow distribute *Point Man* to 100,000 guys across the country.

Back in 1989, I thought I was really pushing the boundaries by asking God to provide 100,000 readers for *Point Man*. Yet, here we are in 1996 and *Point Man* now has over a quarter of a million copies in print. And you know what's really funny. Christian men *are* filling football stadiums. Not just one stadium. Stadiums all over the country. I recently got a call from Promise Keepers asking me to speak in Charlotte and several other cities this year. Guess how many they are expecting in Charlotte. At least 100,000 guys. And some people think that God doesn't have a sense of humor? I think that the Father, the Son and the Holy Spirit must have gotten a pretty good laugh out of my 1989 scrawny prayer (and I say that with reverence). "Now to Him Who is able to do exceeding abundantly beyond anything that you could ever ask or think." That's how Paul put it in Ephesians 3:20.

Now let's make one thing real clear. The only reason I mention these numbers is to give honor to Jesus Christ for what He has done and for what He is doing. It is apparent to everyone (including the secular media) that something unusual is going on among Christian men in America. So what is God doing? And how does that relate to the purpose of this book?

We live in a time when God is doing something on an extraordinary scale. Never before in two thousand years of church history has God worked like He is now working in the lives of men.

My two sons are fourteen and eleven years of age. When they are in their seventies they will tell their grandchildren of the unique time in American history when they attended Promise Keepers events in crowded football stadiums. And their grandchildren will listen in amazement and think that those were the "good old days."

God is up to something that is utterly remarkable. It is absolutely thrilling to sing worship songs to the Lord with sixty thousand other men in a dome designed for football. But we have got to do more than just fill football stadiums. We have got to move from events to *equipping*. That's not to put down the gigantic gatherings. It's simply understanding that we must move to the next level. Men are waking up to their responsibilities. But those men must be equipped and trained to convert that stadium energy into daily commitment to their Lord and their families.

For a number of years, Abe Lemons coached basketball at the University of Texas. Young players have a tendency to get excited only when playing in front of the big crowds. But Lemons drilled into his players the importance of practicing well.

Lemons once said to his players, "You've got to practice *every* day. *One* day of practice is like *one* day of clean living. It doesn't do you any good."

That brings us to the purpose of this book.

This book is designed to amplify and highlight the principles that I wrote about in *Point Man*. I've broken the contents down into forty-five distinct studies that will enable you to actually *practice* the principles that enable a man to be a spiritual leader. You can study on your own or with a group. That's up to you. You can study and practice at your own pace. My personal recommendation would be to take a week for each section. That way you can really focus on those particular areas without feeling you must hurry up and finish. If you aim for one study per week, that will get you through this book in forty-five weeks. If you take a couple of weeks off for vacation — plus the unexpected interruptions in your schedule — it will pretty much take a full year to complete the studies in this book.

If you take it slowly and methodically, and *practice* these principles daily, I can guarantee you that God will do a great work in your life in the next twelve months. The goal of the Christian life is not to grow *old* in Christ. The goal of the Christian life is to grow *up* in Christ. Men who grow *up* in Christ are good practice players. The don't just get excited and pumped up in a stadium full of guys. They know that the real challenge of their spiritual leadership is practicing these principles daily in front of a *small* group of onlookers. And those onlookers are your wife and children.

That's where we really want to excel. In the Christian life, what happens in the stadium will never matter more than what happens at home. The home is the practice field of the Christian life. It's where we play the game for keeps. Home's where the *real* victories take place. And to borrow Max Lucado's term, it's where our practice and diligence in leading our families can bring about "the applause of heaven."

Let's get to work, gentlemen. Dave Branon has done a great job in shaping these practice sessions for us. I think you'll enjoy the ride.

Steve Farrar
January, 1996
Dallas, Texas

UNDER WHOSE COMMAND?

"Unless the Lord watches over the city, the watchmen stand guard in vain" (Psalm 127:1).

MARCHING ORDERS

FROM POINT MAN
Read: Chapter One,
pages 11-20

FROM THE BIBLE
Read: Psalm 127

As you read Psalm 127, think about these questions:

• Obviously God is not in the business of constructing homes, so what is Solomon talking about when he says, "Unless the Lord builds the house?"

• What does "labor in vain" mean? When was a time you labored in vain?

• Can there be any correlation made between verse 2 and the trouble in which our nation's cities find themselves?

• In our hectic work-a-day world, do you find yourself identifying easily with verse 2? The point, however, is not that our work is useless if we work hard and work long hours. Instead, the point is what?

• Verses 3 and 4 run counter to the common thinking in our society about children. How can it rearrange your thinking about your children?

• What is the greatest thing we can do to make sure our children don't put us to shame?

General Norman H. Schwarzkopf stood before the nation with confidence.

The Persian Gulf War was in full swing in early 1991, and the American people wanted to know how their boys were doing against Saddam Hussein's forces. As Schwarzkopf stood behind the podium in his army fatigues, surrounded by charts, maps, and satellite photos, he exuded a calm, secure presence that helped people all across the United States feel assured that victory would be swift and complete.

In a war, the commanding officer sets the tone. It is his plan that the troops must carry out, and it is his expertise that the fighting forces stake their lives on.

In the Persian Gulf War, no matter how well-trained the men and women on the U.S. and coalition forces were, if they had poor commanding officers, victory would not have been guaranteed.

The officer in charge must watch over the battlefield, or the front-line people will battle in vain.

In your role as leader of your family, you are the last line of defense as you guard your kids and wife from the onslaught of the world. If you try to tackle that daunting task alone, you'll lose. You must align yourself under the leadership of the Great Commander. Without God's guidance, assurance, direction, and protection, the enemy will overwhelm you.

Look closely at how vital God's help is in your family, according to Psalm 127.

First, it is the heavenly Father who is the architect and builder of your home (v. 1). His plan for families and for parenting, found throughout Scripture, is flawless. Are you following His plan?

Second, as already mentioned, your only true protection comes from the One who sees everything. Are you entrusting your very life to His will?

Third, your efforts are fruitless unless blessed by the Lord no matter how hard you work. Are you asking God to bless your actions and guide your decisions as you labor in the work force?

Fourth, your children are a blessing that comes directly from God's hand. You can be assured that God will not give you something as a blessing that you cannot maintain as a blessing. When the psalmist says, "Sons are a heritage from the Lord, children a reward from him" (verse 3), you can do little but stand back in amazement.

Imagine. God has given you a reward or prize. He has honored you with children. He says to you, "Here, take this precious child as a gift!"

If you see your children as that important to God, you can easily recognize that He will also give you the provisions and wisdom to help your family honor Him. Do you agree with God that your children are a blessing?

Think of the confidence these four factors can give you! God, who is all-powerful, all-knowing, and everywhere present — the God who has jurisdiction over the whole earth — cares deeply for your little family nestled in your house on your street.

He wants to give you wisdom when your children question you about the importance of Christianity. He wants to provide guidance when you don't know how strict to be with them. In short, He wants to be your commanding officer while you are standing watch over your family.

General Schwarzkopf himself, with all his concern for his fighting men and women, couldn't care nearly as much for his troops as God does for us, his watchmen.

That truth alone should spur you to new commitment to your children, for you know that you will never go into the battle unequipped or unprotected from on high.

It's a war out there. That's for sure. But when your commanding officer is the One who has already been declared the winner, you can't lose.

You are the point man, but God must be the commanding officer.

1. When was the last time I thanked God for my family specifically by name? And have I ever thanked Him for the unique traits that they display — both strengths and weaknesses?

2. What does the second part of Psalm 127:5 mean? How are my children contending with enemies, and what am I doing to make sure they win those battles?

CALL TO ACTION

The next time a key dilemma begins to develop in my family, I will pray for God's guidance and then seek through His Word for an answer. The results of that action:

Dilemma:

_____

God-guided action:

_____

Result:

_____

Dear Lord, thank you for my family. Please protect me from taking them for granted or from being weary of my children because of the pressures of life. Help me to lean on you, my commanding officer, for guidance, wisdom, and strength. Protect my children as we fight the battle together.

KEEPING THE PROMISE

"For this reason a man will leave his father and mother and be united to his wife, and they will become one flesh" (Genesis 2:24).

MARCHING ORDERS

FROM POINT MAN
Read: Chapter One,
pages 20-27

FROM THE BIBLE
Read: Genesis 2:4–25

As you read today's Scripture passage, ask yourself:

• How do you react to verse 7? Do you say, "Hey, that's not what I was taught in school"? Do you say, "Nice story, but it can't be taken literally"? Do you say, "Every time I read how God created us, I'm in awe"? Or some other reaction?

• What difference does it make whether this account is an accurate portrayal of the actual creation of man or only an allegory — a story that has meaning but is not based on fact? How does it affect your reading of the rest of the Bible?

• What is the value of verse 20 to you? How does it affect your relationship with your wife to know that Adam was not complete without Eve?

• If you and your wife are "one flesh," what will this mean to your relationship outside of the sexual ramifications? How should it affect the way you treat her?

There is something a little strange about Genesis 2:24. Think about it.

The story is about two people who don't have parents. Never had them, never would.

They weren't born; they were created. No parents-in-law. No blaming their problems on a bad childhood. Just Adam and his lovely wife Eve.

That's not the weird part. The odd touch in verse 24 is that after the narrative tells about God's creation of Adam and then Eve, we are told, "For this reason a man will leave his father and mother..."

Why bring parents into this if neither of the first couple had them?

Because everyone else would.

Adam and Eve, the prototypical couple, were no different from you and your wife (except that you have parents). Like you, they needed to be devoted completely to each other. Like you, they needed to share the spiritual and physical union that is marriage.

Like you, they had to become one.

And becoming one means clearing the slate of anyone or anything else who might interfere with the union.

That, my friend, is a huge commitment. It is a big promise. It is a serious vow.

Yet that's what you did on the day you stood at the front of the church with knees shaking and sweat staining your rented tux.

Right there in the open, before God and everybody else, you promised that you were about to become one with the luscious lady at your side. You said, in effect, "Thanks Mom and Dad for your help, but I'm detaching myself from you. From now on, I'm going to be hooked up spiritually and physically with your new daughter-in-law."

In effect, although you don't live in Eden or anything remotely resembling it, you are in the same state as Adam and Eve. It was the two of you melding into one being.

Imagine what this means.

First, it means being united (verse 24). Whether this is primarily a sexual meaning or of two hearts joined in love, it suggests a shared commitment.

Second, it means being one flesh. The sexual union of a man and a woman goes far beyond the act. As described in 1 Corinthians 6:12–20, sexuality is closely related to our spirituality.

Third, it means true freedom in sexuality. Although our world tries to make immorality seems as natural as peanut butter, there is a shameful, guilt-filled degradation in an out-of-marriage union never found when a husband and a wife truly enjoy each other sexually.

With Adam and Eve's example in mind, you can take the right action to preserve your relationship with your wife and prevent Satan from tricking you into breaking your promise.

For example, whenever Satan attempts to drive a wedge between the two of you, tell him to get lost because your hearts are eternally joined in love.

It means whenever your wife demonstrates characteristics you might not like, your job is to remain her companion and lover — working in unison to solve the problems while never once entertaining thoughts of reneging on your promise to stay together for better or worse.

It means that no other human relationship — even with your immediate family — should draw you away from your wife.

And it means that if some flirt enters your life flaunting her charms in your direction, you refuse to even think about establishing a relationship with her.

For Adam and Eve, it was simple. First there was just a man. Then there was a man and a woman. And they became one. No competition. No questions.

Create for you and your wife a Eden-like safety net. Together, eliminate any thoughts or actions that might lead you to step out of that net and break your promise to your wife.

And lean on God for protection. It was His idea in the first place to create marriage. Honor Him by keeping your promise.

DEBRIEFING

1. How secure does my wife feel about my promises to stay with her for a lifetime? How confident am I that my marriage is going to stay together?

2. What have I done in the past two weeks to make my marriage Eden-like: united, spiritually unified, sexually pure? What would God have me do to strengthen my vows to my wife and to demonstrate my love?

CALL TO ACTION

Here are three areas I will work on to make sure my wife knows how much I appreciate her and am committed to her:

a: _____

b: _____

c: _____

Dear Lord, thank you for giving me my wife. Thank you for her _____. Thank you that she is good at _____. Thank you that we like to _____ together. Please help me to avoid _____, which could make me think I would want to go back on my promise I made to her. Protect us, Lord. Keep us strong in you and loving toward each other. Help us keep our promise to each other.

DON'T CHASE THEM AWAY

"Fathers, do not exasperate your children..."
(Ephesians 6:4).

MARCHING ORDERS

FROM POINT MAN
Read: Chapter One,
pages 20-21

FROM THE BIBLE
Read: Ephesians 6:1–4

In today's brief Bible reading, don't miss these points:

• In this passage about parents and their children, the first burden is put on the children to obey. Notice, though, that they are to obey "in the Lord," which seems to indicate that the parents are in tune with God when they discipline.

• Children are expected to honor their parents, but again, the passage implies that the parents are honorable in their treatment of their children.

• The contrast in verse 4 is between exasperating the children and bringing them up in the training and instruction of the Lord. Clearly, an exasperating father is not training in a godly manner.

THINKING IT THROUGH

Children are easily exasperated.

If you make them rinse the dishes when they'd rather be out riding their bikes, they can make themselves seem like the most abused children on earth.

They can find reasons to be upset with you when they have to practice the piano on a nice, sunny day (or sometimes even a nasty day). Or when they have to be polite and greet people properly in public. Or when they can't understand why the family doesn't eat all its meals at McDonald's.

As hard as we try, we cannot avoid making rulings that our children disagree with. We cannot avoid coming down on the wrong side of decisions. We cannot avoid occasional dissension in the ranks. We cannot avoid exasperating them.

Yet this is not the kind of exasperation the apostle Paul is talking about in Ephesians 6:4. He's not telling us that we have to have peace at all costs, that we can't stand up to our children, or that we have to let them walk all over us. That's not parenting; that's baby-sitting.

He's talking about the kind of exasperation that will cause serious, long-range problems between us and them. The kind of frustrations we cause our children that make them want to get away from us and not look back. The kind of mistreatment that alienates parents and children for the long term.

He's talking about exasperating them by raising them by other standards than those found in the Bible.

If we try to raise our children without "the training and instruction of the Lord," we will most probably frustrate them so much they'll want out of the situation.

Let's visit a school classroom to find an analogy for this thinking. Actually, we'll visit two classrooms.

Classroom One: Mrs. Hardinfair presiding. On the first day of school, she sets in motion a clear set of guidelines — all within the bounds of the school's discipline procedures. She makes no apologies for the rules, and she lets her students know that she expects them to obey. Mrs. Hardinfair doesn't smile a lot at first, and unlike others, she assigns homework the first day. Each day in her classroom is full of instruction, challenges, and educational activities.

In the beginning, students grumble and seem exasperated

with her relentless pursuit of excellence. One by one, though, as she interacts with them, they understand that she cares enough to expect good things of them.

By the end of the year, all but the most rebellious students are talking about what a great teacher Mrs. Hardinfair is. She seemed so exasperating at first, but in the end, proved to be a remarkably popular teacher.

Classroom Two: Mr. Barelythere presiding. Twenty minutes into the first class of the year, the students know they have him right where they want him. He lets them sit where they want, he doesn't have any classroom rules, and he doesn't stop them from having little sidebars with classmates as he is talking.

Day by day as the students go to class, the uproar in the room gets louder and louder. Frustrated, Mr. Barelythere resorts to showing a lot of movies in class and requiring very little work. Students run the show, and know they can get away with anything.

Once the end of the year rolled around, though, they were the most frustrated students in the school. They knew they hadn't learned much in the class, and the fun of seeing Mr. Barelythere get angry and yell at them wore off. At the end, the students even began to feel sorry for him. But they were sorrier that they had wasted a whole year in a subject they needed to grasp. Soon they began hearing rumors that next year Mr. Barelythere would be not there at all. And no one was too sad about that.

Exasperating parenting is like that. It is weak, uncommitted, unchallenging parenting that seeks the easy way out, yet leads to nothing but trouble.

Bringing our children up in the training and instruction of the Lord, on the other hand, may seem more difficult. Yet the end product is better. It's a task that calls for discipline on our part to stick to biblical guidelines. It calls for courage to make tough decisions. It calls for caring enough to make sure we set a pattern of loving, compassionate teaching.

But what is the "training and instruction of the Lord" that this verse refers to? Here are some examples, directly from God's Word.

1. *Attitudes from the Beatitudes.* Jesus clearly told us how we should view our condition, how we should view others, and what he expects of us in Matthew 5:1–10. Beatitude attitudes can help us as we train our children.

2. *Fruit at the root.* Further instruction in what kinds of people we should be and what kind of persons we want our children to be is found in Galatians 5:22–23. If we can encourage this kind of fruit in our children, we'll not exasperate them.

3. *Savior behavior.* Basic to any instruction in the Lord is making sure that those we instruct are believers in Jesus Christ. Beyond that, we need to investigate Jesus' life with our children to see how He lived as an example to us.

4. *Look in the book.* For further guidelines for Christian living, we need to study the Bible, especially the New Testament. Passages like Ephesians 4:17–5:21, Galatians 5:13–26, Philippians 4:8, and Colossians 3:1–17 can give you the specifics you need as you instruct.

The further we get from God's teaching, the more we will frustrate our children. And the further we get from God, the less likely we will be to teach our children without provoking them and sending them away from us.

A godly character and instruction based on God's Word — those two essential elements will help us be dads who don't chase our children away.

MOTTO

Successful parenting depends on good guidelines and a good teacher.

1. Have I ever sat down to delineate the specific biblical guidelines I want my children to follow?

2. Is my attitude toward my children laissez-faire or involved? Which would be more frustrating for them?

3. When are some times I have exasperated my children in the wrong way? What could I change to avoid doing that again?

CALL TO ACTION

1. Here are five biblical guidelines I think are important for my children to live by: _____

_____

_____

_____

2. What situation has most recently caused dad-child dissension in the family? _____

How did I handle that situation?_____

_____

What biblical guideline would help me handle it better?

_____

_____

_____

Dear heavenly Father, thank you for my children. I don't want to chase them away with bad fathering, so please help me to bring them up your way. Help me to understand how your Word, the Bible, can guide my instruction of them. Give me your wisdom to be the right kind of dad.

THE TEMPTATION

"No temptation has seized you except what is common to man. And God is faithful; he will not let you be tempted beyond what you can bear. But when you are tempted, he will also provide a way out so that you can stand up under it" (1 Corinthians 10:13).

MARCHING ORDERS

FROM POINT MAN
Read: Chapter One,
pages 27-30

FROM THE BIBLE
Read: 2 Samuel 11

As you read 2 Samuel 11, think about these questions:

• What was David's first mistake? After he stepped out on the roof and spied Bathsheba, what should he have done?

• What does his sending someone to "find out about her" and later sending "messengers to get her" reveal about David in that stage of his life?

• What biblical passage about the results of sin comes to mind when you read verse 5?

• Compare the character of David with the character of Uriah, as revealed in verses 8–13. Which one would you put in the faith hall of fame in Hebrews 11?

• David proceeded to come up with one of the most hateful schemes imaginable, and it resulted in his getting the desired result. Notice, however, the last words of the chapter: "But the thing David had done displeased the Lord." That legacy is life's most difficult.

Another day of being king had taken its toll on David. Not long before, he had sent his troops off to fight and die in the wars against the hated Ammonites. Although the king had stayed behind out of battle-harm's way, surely the weight of responsibility rested awkwardly and heavily on his shoulders.

Perhaps it was a fitful rest that caused him to take an evening stroll on the flat rooftop of the palace. Maybe he thought the clear cool air would ease his mind and help him sort out the commands that the next day would demand.

The man was under pressure. Ruling a country and running a long-distance war can do that.

So can running a business. Or keeping a boss happy at the shop. Or filling orders as quickly as possible on the line. Or painting houses to the contractor's and the homeowner's satisfaction. Or balancing the books of a small business.

We all face pressure. We all seek something to take our minds of the struggles of work and the battles at home. We all would love an escape.

There are so many ways we can get that little respite we need.

We can take a walk (which is what David did).

We can crash in front of Monday Night Football.

We can take our wife out for a nice dinner. In fact, it doesn't even have to be a fancy one. A trip to McDonald's can give us the break we deserve.

We can play a round of golf. Of course, that might lead to frustrations of a different kind.

We can grab a good book and find a quiet place to read.

Or we can find a woman whose wiles we cannot resist.

Don't be shocked. It is an option. And it is the method David decided on during this spring evening of his discontent.

For us, the temptation is certainly out there. Women are on the horizon, some willing to fulfill the kind of fantasy desires that men think will bring them the escape they desire.

Whatever ran through David's mind that evening when he spied Bathsheba and convinced himself that he should have her, he certainly didn't foresee the trouble his decision was going to cause him.

None of us ever do.

For David, his yielding to temptation led to the following consequences:

• Bathsheba became pregnant.

• When David tried to cover up his paternity, Bathsheba's husband signed his own death warrant by refusing to cooperate.

• David committed cold-blooded murder of the loyal soldier by sticking him on the front lines.

• The baby Bathsheba bore David died.

• In David's own words, speaking of the time between his sin and his confession of it to God, "When I kept silent, my bones wasted away through my groaning all day long. For day and night your hand was heavy upon me; my strength was sapped" (Psalm 32:3–4).

David's sin on that cool spring evening followed him the rest of his life. The temptation led to sin, which led to great trouble.

Like David, each of us faces temptation. Yet none of us ever has to live with the consequences of temptation. We don't have to ask forgiveness for temptation. Temptation doesn't wreck homes and throw people on life's trash heap.

What causes the problems for us is giving in to temptation.

Our Lord Jesus himself faced temptation — and overcame it. Satan tried to get Jesus to sin, but He refused to give in. That is our goal.

To do what Jesus did in the face of temptation, we have to understand a couple of things that David failed to recognize on that fateful night when he sought an escape and found a trap.

First, we need to ask God to protect us from temptation. Although as we've said, temptation is not sin, we are pretty easy marks for it — good intentions and all. Jesus told Peter this: "Watch and pray so that you will not fall into temptation. The spirit is willing, but the body is weak" (Matthew 26:41). We may try to convince ourselves that we can look temptation in the face and scare it away, but we need divine help to do that. And sometimes our own drives overpower our dependence on the Holy Spirit.

Therefore, Jesus was suggesting to Peter that his first priority was to avoid temptation — not take a chance that it might overpower him.

Second, the converse is true. If we let temptation overpower us, it is because we are not depending on God. According to 1 Corinthians 10:13, what David faced and what we face are no different. Sexual temptation is "common to man." We are no more tempted than anyone else. But if we keep in fellowship with God, he will faithfully lead us out of the temptation and into righteousness.

Only when we cut off God's help will we fall.

That's what David did, and look at the price he paid.

MOTTO

It's not a sin to face temptation, only to give in to it.

DEBRIEFING

1. What are the three top temptations I face? When was the last time I prayed that God would protect me from them?

2. Do I ever invite temptation? What do I say to convince myself that it's okay to flirt with sin?

3. Have I ever stopped to thank God for the many times He has protected me from giving in to a temptation that could ruin my marriage? What do I learn about God when I think of how He helps me in this area of my life?

CALL TO ACTION

When I next face a temptation, I will take these three steps before I do anything else:
1. Stop immediately and ask God for help.
2. Think through all the consequences.
3. Run!

Dear Father, thank you for warning us about the consequences of sin through the story of David. Please lead me not into temptation, but deliver me from evil. I ask your Spirit to protect me from giving in to temptations throughout this day. Prompt me to ask this of you each day.

A MODEL SON

"But Daniel resolved not to defile himself with the royal food and wine..." (Daniel 1:8).

MARCHING ORDERS

FROM POINT MAN
Read: Chapter Two,
pages 31-34

FROM THE BIBLE
Read: Daniel 1

Here are some possible headlines from today's Scripture passage:

• Daniel, Friends Become Prisoners Of War

• Teens Of Noble Birth Brought Before The King

• King Plans To Retrain Young Men

• Daniel Stands Ground; Gets God's Blessing

• The Daniel Three Pass Huge Test

• King Finds No Equal To Daniel Trio

THINKING IT THROUGH

Imagine what kind of dad Daniel must have had.

Not always, but most of the time, you can tell what a dad is like by looking at his son.

You see it often with athletes. Boys whose dads are coaches are often the most disciplined, the quickest to pick up new concepts, the most likely to be the team leaders. They seem like natural leaders.

The 1993 Heisman Trophy winner, Charlie Ward, for instance, is the son of a coach. As is point guard extraordinaire Mark Price. They learned leadership at their fathers' feet.

Daniel would have made a great quarterback. He was good-looking, which may not help a guy call plays and rifle passes, but it comes in handy after the game. He was gifted in wisdom. He was knowledgeable. He was a quick study.

But what made Daniel stand out in this story has nothing to do with his natural attributes. For those of us who have passed the time when we could get by on our youthful good looks and quick wit, that's good news. Daniel's key trait was his brave adherence to right action in the face of pressure (see, I told you he'd make a good quarterback).

The king of the entire domain wanted Daniel to snack on the royal goodies, food that was probably more delectable than any Daniel had ever seen. For some reason, however, those delicacies prepared in the king's kitchen were not on God's menu. The text says, "But Daniel resolved not to defile himself with the royal food and wine, and he asked the chief official for permission not to defile himself this way."

If I know anything about teenagers, they generally don't go around defying the king. They may seem a bit rebellious at times, but often they can't even stand up to each other when an issue of right and wrong is a stack, let alone face down the king. That's where I think Daniel's upbringing comes into play.

Someone, somewhere, had taught the lad that certain foods were off limits if he wanted to please God. Even when the pressure was on, he didn't lose his head. Well, he could have lost his head if the king had become angry, but fortunately Nebuchadnezzar had some scruples.

What we wouldn't give to have sons and daughters who would do what Daniel did!

What we wouldn't do to save our children from a world that is trying to defile them in so many ways.

What we wouldn't do to help them know that defiling themselves leads only to sorrow and trouble.

The first chapter of Daniel doesn't give any clues as to how Daniel's parents helped him achieve his strength of character, but it does reveal some characteristics we must instill in our boys and girls if we want to save them from enemies far worse than Nebuchadnezzar.

First, we must empower them with the joy of learning. Daniel and his friends showed an "aptitude for every kind of learning." They had obviously received instruction in many disciplines in a way that piqued their interest. As dads, one of the most vital things we can do for our sons and daughters is to give them wide-ranging educational experiences — whether through books, computers, traveling, or simply sharing our knowledge with them. We need to search out their aptitudes and then help develop them.

Second, we must ensure that our children are well-informed, as were Daniel and his friends. There are so many errors they can learn if we leave the teaching to the wrong people. Areas such as evolution, sexuality, religion, and so many other fields are rifled with error. Our task is to either teach them correctly or make sure they have access to right teaching in these areas.

Third, we need to encourage our children to keep their relationship with God strong. When we read that "God gave knowledge and understanding" to Daniel, we know that he and God were on speaking terms. The lines of communication were already open between the two when Daniel went into the king's court, they stayed open when Daniel did what was right in God's eyes, and that openness was rewarded with additional blessings.

Perhaps you cannot imagine what it would be like to be Daniel's dad. But you are your children's dad. With God's guiding hand, prepare your children for the day when they will have to stand before a challenge without your help. Using Daniel's model, let's make every effort to prepare them now for what lies ahead. That's how we'll save our boys and girls.

MOTTO

Challenging our children now helps them face life's challenges later.

DEBRIEFING

1. What do I see as the biggest challenges my children will face when they go out on their own? What am I doing now to prepare them mentally and spiritually?

2. My son or daughter seems already to be heading down a path I don't like, and I feel it is too late to turn him or her around. Where can I turn for help?

3. What help does God offer me in my task as a parent? What of His characteristics or teachings should I hold onto right now as I seek to save my children?

CALL TO ACTION

1. I will pray for my children for five minutes each day. I will do this at what time each day?

2. Here are five specific biblical principles I will try to instill in my children as I interact with them:

a. _____

b. _____

c. _____

d. _____

e. _____

Father, you are the perfect dad. You know I need your guidance to help save my children from a world that wants to destroy them. Please give me strength for the task, wisdom to know what to do, knowledge to teach them the right thing, and spiritual discernment to direct them with biblical teaching. Help me to make every day an opportunity to bring them closer to you.

THE PERFECT GAME

"How can a young man keep his way pure? By living according to your Word" (Psalm 119:9).

Don't miss the significance of today's Bible reading:

• The first part of verse 9 is a specific call for purity that should perk the ears of every father because of its promise.

• Following that promise is a list of nine activities that will lead a young man in the right path.

One of the most rare accomplishments in baseball is the perfect game. Only a handful of times in more than a century of professional baseball has a major league pitcher faced twenty-seven hitters and gotten them all out without a runner reaching first base.

A perfect game takes the cooperation of a number of people. The pitcher, of course, has to have his best stuff. The fielders have to play flawlessly — and sometimes heroically. The umpires have to make the right calls. The manager has to position the players correctly in the field. It is a confluence of good baseball that seldom occurs.

Pitching a perfect game is one of only two situations in which a pitcher who throws a complete game is assured of a victory. The other is a shutout. In either case, he must win or he will not receive credit for either a perfect game or a shutout.

But he doesn't have to do either to win the game. He can pitch a no-hitter or a one-hitter. He can allow several hits. He can allow lots of hits, walks, and runs.

In other words, it is a great feat to pitch a perfect game — or even a shutout — but it is not necessary to be a winner.

It's a good thing life is like that, because in the history of the world, only one Person was ever perfect.

The rest of us have to stumble along with no-hitters, or more generally, multi-hit games full of errors.

Yet, despite our poor record, we have encouraging promises for our sons like the one in Psalm 119:9. Here David details for us how a young man can *keep* his way pure. It suggests that for the young man who already has a good streak going (like a guy pitching a perfect game), there are some guidelines to keep purity a priority for him.

As fathers, this is a hot-button item. We want our sons to be pure and stay pure in their living habits. We are like the manager who is trying to coax his pitcher's way through an outstanding outing on the mound. We want to give the right advice that will keep our sons heading toward purity.

So we need to reach in our back pocket and pull out the rule book to see what it says in Psalm 119:9–16.

To keep pure a young man must:
• live according to God's Word.

• seek God with a whole heart.

• not stray from God's commands.

• hide God's Word in his heart to keep from sin.

- learn God's decrees.

- follow God's guidelines with rejoicing.

- meditate on God's standards.

- take delight in God's guidelines.

- never neglect the Word of God.

We are raising the next generation of fathers and mothers, and one of the most profound needs our society has is for pure young people to come along and take the leadership.

Statistics I've seen suggest that the number of young people who are winning — much less pitching perfect games — is shrinking. The task of growing up to become leaders is going to be tough for our children.

Consequently, the pressure is on us as Christian dads to both instruct and model purity for our children. We cannot expect them to rise to any standard close to perfection until we first demonstrate it for them. So we need to reach into that back pocket again and ask ourselves if we are following Psalm 119:9-16 ourselves:

•Do we conduct our business and family practices by biblical guidelines? Are we honest and above-board in all of our dealings with people?

•Do we seek God with our whole heart? Is trying to know Him better a daily activity?

•Are we memorizing Scripture? It's easy to stop doing that at this stage in life, yet the demands of life would suggest we need more of God's Word in our hearts, not less.

•Do we thank God for His clear teachings and praise him by honoring all such teaching?

•Do we make the Scriptures our constant companion?

This idea of raising not-so-perfect, yet as-pure-as-possible children is a teamwork effort. A pitcher cannot expect to go out to the mound and pitch a perfect game without the support of his whole team. And we cannot expect our children to face a hostile world alone and come out pure.

That's why they need us. They need (1) our guidance to help them know and understand Scriptural guidelines, (2) our good example as a template for their behavior, and (3) our encouragement that they can win.

Walter Johnson never pitched a perfect game. He pitched for twenty-one years in the American League for Washington, yet he was never perfect. Not once in the 802 times that he went out to pitch did he keep every opposing batter off first base. Yet don't feel sorry for him. He won 416 times. Not perfect, but very good.

That's what we want from our children as they grow into adulthood and into the responsibility of raising the next generation. They won't be perfect, but they can strive for purity — a goal they can reach with good teaching and a good example.

MOTTO

Purity is possible.

DEBRIEFING

1. How would I define a pure life as lived by a young person? How does that differ, if at all, from the pure life of an adult?

2. How valuable is my example to my children as they seek a life of purity?

3. Do I feel a heavy sense of responsibility in this regard, or do I think things will pretty much take care of themselves?

CALL TO ACTION

1. What anti-purity messages are being sent into our house through the media? What should I do to tone down the influence of those messages?

2. These are five areas of purity I want to pursue for myself and talk over with my children:

a. _____

b. _____

c. _____

d. _____

e. _____

Dear God, please help me to set the example of right living for my children. Keep me in your Word so your teachings are fresh each day. Guide me to an understanding how best to relay your teachings to my children. Thank you for your help and for your gift of Jesus Christ, in whose salvation alone we can even think about pure lives.

IN THE CARPENTER'S SHOP

*"So he got up, took the child and his mother during
the night and left for Egypt..."* (Matthew 2:14).

MARCHING ORDERS

FROM POINT MAN
Read: Chapter Two,
pages 35-40

FROM THE BIBLE
Read: Matthew 2

Here's a synopsis:

•When King Herod found out that some wise men were nosing around about a new king who had been born, the king was a bit put out.

•Herod hauled the wise men into his court and lied to them, sending them to find the newborn king and, ostensibly, suggesting that he wanted worship him. Kill him was more like it.

•Herod was threatened by Jesus' presence, so he ordered all boys in Bethlehem to be murdered.

•When Joseph heard about this during a dreamy visit by an angel, he took Jesus and Mary and headed to Egypt.

•Later, another angel told Joseph to head for Israel, where he and his family finally settled down safely in Nazareth.

THINKING IT THROUGH

Whenever we think we have it tough as a dad, we need to read about everything Joseph went through as Jesus' earthly father.

That should cure us from feeling sorry for ourselves while also giving us a model of what fatherhood is really all about.

Joseph was a God-fearing Jewish carpenter of little renown, quietly going about his business in the Galilean village of Nazareth. Then one day he got the shock of his life. He discovered his fiancée, Mary, was pregnant.

Embarrassed, Joseph wanted to hide her away. He knew he wasn't the father, and he probably didn't want anyone to think he was. Socially, he had a major crisis on his hands.

Yet he didn't run. He didn't hide. He took the incredible words of an angel at face value — the child was not conceived illegitimately.

Yet that wasn't the only crisis to come. For the next few years, Joseph would find himself at the center of danger. Shortly after Jesus was born in Bethlehem, his life was threatened, forcing Joseph and his tiny family to take off for Egypt. Imagine having to flee for fear that soldiers would kill your child.

Still later, Joseph's family was uprooted again when they were told by an angel to return to his hometown of Nazareth. Finally, the ordeal was over, and Joseph, Mary, and Jesus could live the normal life that Joseph had at first envisioned when he became betrothed to Mary.

Joseph is to be admired. He could have checked out of this situation any number of times. He could have reasoned early on that this was Mary's problem, not his. Who knows what kind of embarrassment he faced as he took care of Mary during her pregnancy.

And later, when he knew that soldiers were after the young boy, he could have abandoned them and headed for safety.

Guys do it all the time. They face a bit of a struggle in the relationship — whether with a wife that has done something not of his liking or with children who seem to be too much trouble — and they run. Afraid to tackle the problems that are a part of nurturing a family, they grab their gear, hop in the sports utility car, and run.

Joseph stuck to his God-ordained job — taking care of Mary and Jesus under adverse circumstances.

And because he did, just look at the advantage he gained and the help he could be to Jesus. His loyalty enabled him to be the guardian, father, and teacher of the greatest Teacher ever born.

It gave him the opportunity to share his carpenter's workshop with the Creator. Imagine the joy of showing the One who created the forests how to make a chair. Think of the challenge of asking the One who flung the worlds in place to sweep up the cuttings on the shop floor.

The boy Jesus, of course, did not grow up to be a carpenter like Joseph. He grew up to astound people with his wisdom. On one occasion, when he was teaching people in Nazareth, his listeners were amazed. Incredulously, they asked, "Where did this man get his wisdom and these miraculous powers? ...Isn't this the carpenter's son?" (Matthew 13:54–55).

Indeed, he was. Joseph could not take credit for the miraculous powers or wisdom of this one who was both God and man, but he could take credit for sticking by his boy. Had he run like so many do, Jesus would not have been noted as "the carpenter's son."

Is something threatening to drive you away from the family God gave you? Perhaps, like Joseph's, the family isn't the perfect one you had envisioned. But God is calling you to protect them and build for them a sanctuary.

Beyond that, when people say, "Isn't that the accountant's son?" or "Isn't that the plant foreman's daughter?", will they then notice how you have taught them — how you have shared your life with them on a daily basis to bring them wisdom and knowledge?

God has placed you in your family for a reason. He doesn't want you ever to abandon it — either by running away or by neglecting the opportunity to spend time with your sons or daughters.

It may not be in a carpenter's shop, but find some place and some time when you can share your knowledge and wisdom with your children.

DEBRIEFING

1. Right now I am facing some tough times because of my family. For instance, it's tough because _____.
My choices are to stay and work it through or to abandon what God has given me. What do I need from God right now to see me through the crisis?

2. How many hours a week do I spend with my children, having them learn from me some valuable skills? Is that enough? If not, where can I cut back to give them time? What knowledge or skills should I share with them?

3. In what way can the picture of family presented in Psalm 128 be an incentive for me?

CALL TO ACTION

Whenever I feel like abandoning my post in my family, I will remember these five reasons I cannot desert them:

a._____

b._____

c._____

d._____

e._____

Dear God, right now I'm struggling because of some tough times at home. Please give me the courage to battle the problem and not look for an escape. Remind me of your love, care, and help as I face the task ahead. Thank you for your example of never leaving me or forsaking me.

A TRIP TO THE MOUNTAINS

*"Then God said, 'Take your son, your only son, Isaac,
whom you love, and ... [s]acrifice him there as a
burnt offering...'"* (Genesis 22:2).

MARCHING ORDERS

FROM POINT MAN
Read: Chapter Two,
pages 41-45

FROM THE BIBLE
Read: Genesis 22:1-19

As you read through Genesis 22, think
about these questions:
- Why would God test Abraham?
- What special meaning can you find
in verse 2, which says, "Take your son,
your only son"?
- Three days on the road — what do
you think Abraham and Isaac talked about all that time?

- What is the significance of Abraham's statement to his servants, "We will worship and *then we will come back to you*"?

- What was Abraham's reward for his faith?

THINKING IT THROUGH

For nearly 100 years, Abraham had waited for a son.
When the boy finally came, he was a miracle — born to a
mother ridiculously far past her childbearing years.
An only child. An only son.
He must have been the joy of Abraham's heart.
Surely Abraham could see all his hopes and dreams for the

future wrapped up in Isaac, who would one day rule over Abraham's substantial household.

Then Abraham got a startling call from God. The patriarch had received some incredible messages from Jehovah, including instructions to leave his homeland to travel to an unknown land and word that his wife would conceive in her old age. But this was the most astonishing and the most difficult of all.

This message was bad news indeed. It was a word from God that threatened to destroy all the dreams Abraham could have dreamed as he watched Isaac grow.

"Take your son, your only son Isaac, whom you love, and go to the region of Moriah," God began. "Sacrifice him there as a burnt offering on one of the mountains I will tell you about."

What Scripture records next is one of the most remarkable demonstrations of faith you will ever see.

We are not told of a human-divine war of words.

We are not told of a son-father argument.

We are not told of a mother pleading for her son.

We are told simply, "Early the next morning Abraham got up and saddled his donkey."

That is obedience we cannot fathom. Abraham simply did as he was told. He saddled up his donkey, summoned two servants and his son, cut wood for the sacrifice, and was on his way.

For the next three days, Abraham and Isaac shared what must have been the strangest journey ever. Abraham knew what he was about to do, but Isaac apparently didn't. It wasn't until the two of them had arrived at the place of sacrifice that Isaac said anything about the missing sacrifice.

Abraham loved his son. His son trusted him. Together they must have shared some great conversations on the road to the place of sacrifice.

We can imagine Abraham reminiscing a bit about the months before Isaac's birth, reminding the son how much they wanted him. We can imagine how Isaac must have looked up to

Abraham, for he was a man of both great wealth and great faith. We can picture Abraham reminding Isaac with tears in his eyes that the line of the family would come through the young man — and that his offspring would be great. After all, Abraham had been promised that "through Isaac . . . your offspring will be reckoned" (Hebrews 11:18). The two must have constituted a great mutual admiration society.

Yet, burning in Abraham's heart as the small entourage plodded its way toward an unrevealed place of sacrifice was the knowledge that his son was about to die at his own hands — unless God provided a miracle.

With no guarantees other than the promise of God to guide him along, Abraham did what he was commanded — trusting that somehow God could reconcile what seemed to be two contradictory situations. How could God make Isaac the offspring if he were sacrificed, short of raising him from the dead? And how could Abraham continue to obey God Most High if he didn't sacrifice Isaac?

Abraham faced the ultimate fathering test. Yet, in a sense, it is not too different from the one you as a dad face. You are called to raise your children to give them up. No, not to give them up as physical sacrifices, but to give them up to do what God wants them to do.

As you head toward the day when you have to turn them over to the task God has called them to do, are you confident that God can handle whatever they face? Or do you feel you need to hold on to them as long as possible?

God had a plan for Isaac, and although the circumstances seemed to suggest that plan was nullified, God's miracle worked things out. Likewise, God has a plan for your children. Instruct them, train them, lead them, spend time with them. Then let them go. God will provide for them just as He did for Isaac.

Trusting God means obeying Him without question.

1. What has God asked me to do in the past week that seemed a bit too difficult for me to do? Should I reconsider it now?

2. When have I taken the time to spend with my children, just to get to know them and what makes them tick? Short of taking a three-day journey by donkey, what can I do?

3. How much trust is there between my children and me? Would they trust me in a situation like the one Abraham and Isaac found themselves in? How can I win back or keep our trust intact?

CALL TO ACTION

1. This week, I will set aside _____ hours to take my son/daughter _____ so we can have some time together.

2. My son/daughter and I will spend some time in Genesis 22, talking about father-child trust, our faith in God, and our commitment to do the right thing.

Dear Jehovah-Jirah, you provided a lamb for Abraham; you provided the Lamb of God for me. Please help me to trust that you will always provide what I need. Help me also to build up the trust between my children and me. When my next trial comes, help me to have faith in you.

ONE RIGHTEOUS MAN:

THREE RIGHTEOUS SONS

"By faith Noah, when warned about things not yet seen, in holy fear built an ark to save his family. By his faith he condemned the world and became heir of the righteousness that comes by faith" (Hebrews 11:7).

MARCHING ORDERS

FROM POINT MAN
Read: Chapter Two,
pages 45-51

FROM THE BIBLE
Read: Genesis 6

As you read today's Scripture passage, ask yourself:

• What was the state of things on the earth as this story opens?

• How was God able to pick out Noah so readily? What does this tell us about Noah's relationship with God?

• How did Noah respond to God's call to him in regard to the ark and the coming flood?

THINKING IT THROUGH

Are you familiar with the Pete Maravich story? In the early 1970s, Pistol Pete burst on the basketball scene as the most prolific scorer in college hoops history. For his three years of college ball (freshmen couldn't play on the varsity back then), Maravich averaged more than forty points a game. Incredibly, he had several games in which he scored more than sixty points.

And it wasn't just his shooting that turned Maravich into college basketball's number one attraction. He had developed his ball-handling skills to such a degree that he became something of a magician with the ball.

Pete Maravich, in many ways, changed the way basketball was played. He introduced a level of ball-handling wizardry that influenced young players nationwide to learn new moves. Today many of those fancy moves are standard fare for basketball players. But not until Pete came along and showed that they work, did anyone actually play that way.

But it wasn't really Pete who changed the game.

It was his dad, Press. Press was a former semi-pro player who turned to coaching as a profession. When Pete was just a little boy, Press began to impress on him that he could change the game if he took it to a higher level. It was Press' dream that basketball be taken far beyond the push shot and the simple pass that he grew up with.

Pete Maravich's legacy is secure as one of the greatest innovators in basketball history. And that legacy is a direct result of his father's influence.

In that case, a sports-loving man changed the game of basketball through his teaching and his son.

In Genesis 6, we see how a God-loving man changed the whole world through his faith and through his sons. This legacy-maker was Noah, who was called "a righteous man, blameless among the people..." (Genesis 6:9).

The problem in Noah's day was global corruption. Violence filled the earth. Yet Noah was willing to go against the flow. He did what no one else was doing; he obeyed God's teachings and "walked with God." And, apparently, he left that same legacy with his sons.

When Noah was rewarded for his faithfulness by being named the captain of the only seafaring ship that could outlast the coming flood that God was to send in judgment, his sons were named first mates.

Noah's righteousness left a legacy that ran through his sons and on into the new race of people who populated the earth after the flood.

Because he obeyed God, Noah's influence has continued down through human history.

Press Maravich changed basketball through his son. Noah changed world history through his boys. What legacy should we leave?

Go back to the time of the ark. Notice two things that Noah taught his boys by example: righteousness (Genesis 6:9) and obedience (Genesis 6:22).

Righteousness. As dads, we can do no better than to seek righteousness as our children observe us. Let's see what the Bible says about the reward of being righteous.

The righteous give generously (Psalm 37:21).

The righteous rejoice in the Lord (Psalm 64:10).

The righteous man utters wisdom (Psalm 37:30).

The home of the righteous is blessed (Proverbs 3:33).

The prospect of the righteous is joy (Proverbs 10:28).

God hears the prayer of the righteous (Proverbs 15:29, James 5:16).

The righteous are as bold as a lion (Proverbs 28:1).

We can pass along these and many other traits to our children if we are righteous.

Obedience. Our guideline for living right and teaching our children the right path must come from Scripture. That is a legacy that we can use, then pass along to our children.

Everything falls in line behind the twin legacies of godly righteousness and godly obedience. We may think that a legacy of riches or business acumen or even sports expertise are the greatest things we can pass along to our children.

Press Maravich, late in life, discovered that although his legacy through Pete was important, he had left out a key ingredient — godliness. He discovered it when Pete, who had wasted much of his life on ungodly living, turned his life over to Jesus Christ after his career ended. When he explained his faith to his father, he too accepted Jesus.

Toward the end of his life, Pete toured the country leaving a new legacy. He told young basketball fans everywhere that his basketball trophies, his basketball earnings, and his basketball honors meant absolutely nothing in comparison to his faith in Jesus Christ and his life of obedience to him.

When he died at age forty, he had left two legacies — basketball and spiritual greatness.

What legacy does God want us to leave for our children?

MOTTO

If we cannot model righteousness and obedience, we are leaving the wrong legacy.

DEBRIEFING

1. If I were to ask my children right now what legacy I am leaving in their life, what would they say?

2. If God were looking for a righteous man today to save the world, would he look twice at me or just pass me by? What do I need to do to be more righteous?

3. What can I do this week to make the legacy I leave my children lean more toward righteousness and obedience?

CALL TO ACTION

1. Perhaps it would be good to trace my legacy. What did my grandfather teach my father? What did my father teach me?

2. In a secure place I will write the legacy I want to leave my children.

Lord, please cleanse me of anything that would make me be more like the wicked people of Noah's day than like Noah. Instruct me in righteousness and obedience, and let my children see the progress in my life.

SO WHAT'S THE BIG DEAL?

"It is God's will that you should be sanctified: that you should avoid sexual immorality…" (1 Thessalonians 4:3).

MARCHING ORDERS

FROM POINT MAN
Read: Chapter Three,
pages 53-60

FROM THE BIBLE
Read: 1 Corinthians
6:12–20

In today's brief Bible reading, don't miss these points:

•Notice how clearly 1 Corinthians 6:13 contradicts the philosophy of our society in regard to sexual activity.

•Verses 15 and 16 are startling in their ramifications. The picture is not one we want to think about, but it suggests a very sacrilegious act on the part of a Christian who commits sexual sin.

•Consider how a sexual sin is a sin against a person's own body. Think about how that relates to all the physical problems promiscuous sex is causing.

THINKING IT THROUGH

Basketball, baseball, football, and sex. In what way are these four things connected? They are the top four sports in America today.

The Super Bowl may get the highest TV rating of any true sporting event, but sex on TV gets a lot more air time — and is seemingly winning the ratings wars. From sitcoms in what used to be the family hour to sleazy pseudo-news programs like *Hard Copy* and *Extra* to daytime soaps to commercials to the crude and rude talk shows, TV is promoting sex more than Monday Night Football, the NBA Finals, March Madness, and the World Series all put together.

Apparently, Christians are buying into this new approach to sex. Several of Christendom's top music stars have thrown away incredible ministries because they decided to play the sex game. Pastors by the hundreds have fallen from grace in the past decade because they wanted to get off the sidelines and get into the sex action. And Christians by the thousands spend time and money to watch TV programs and movies that glorify bedroom escapades.

So, what's the big deal? Is sex all that bad that we have to get all bent out of shape about it? After all, God invented it. What harm does it do to have a little bit of fun? And, hey, if you protect yourself, nobody's going to get hurt, right?

Not if we believe God's Word. If we take Scriptures seriously, we cannot have a cavalier attitude toward sex. We cannot look at it as a sporting event. We cannot even begin to fool around with it outside of the boundaries so clearly spelled out in the Bible.

For a subject so seemingly delicate, the Bible has a surprisingly large volume of passages on the subject. If we would look at these passages closely, we can draw some clear conclusions as to why our sexual activity is such a big deal to God.

1. *We were created to glorify God; we were not created for sexual immorality* (1 Corinthians 6:13). Any time you use something for a purpose other than what it was intended for, you are asking for trouble. Using your shoe for a hammer wrecks the sole. Using your car key to pry something open bends it out of shape. Using a friend to gain personal favors destroys a relationship. Using sex for excitement outside of marriage fouls up your life, the life of the other person, and the lives of everyone else you know. And besides, it opens you up to a broad listing of diseases — both

physical and psychological. God wasn't trying to spoil our fun with this principle, but to protect us from damage.

2. *When a Christian unites with another in sexual sin, he unites the sacred with the pagan* (1 Corinthians 6:15–16). The Holy Spirit does not take a vacation when a man who professes to be a child of God commits sexual sin. He is right there, being grieved. Imagine it. To perform sexual sin, we have to take God with us. That is indeed a humbling thought.

3. *Committing sexual sin is self-damaging* (1 Corinthians 6:18). Look at all the ways immoral sex damages a man. It leaves him with a guilt that will eat away at him. It destroys his relationship with his spouse, no matter how hard he tries to think otherwise. And perhaps most damaging, it harms his fellowship with God.

4. *Sexual sin is never God's will for you* (1 Thessalonians 4:3–8). Incredibly, those who counsel Christians have to deal with this question quite often. Folks fall in love with someone they are not married to, and they discover that their sexual desire is greater for the non-spouse. They take that as a sign that God is blessing the new relationship, so they feel that it is God's will for them to disunite with their spouse and unite in sexual activity with their newfound love.

Not so, this passage indicates. Part of being holy, it says, is to avoid sexual immorality by controlling the body, by avoiding heathen-like passionate lust, by being careful not to take advantage of someone else — which is what adultery always consists of.

Our God is a God of love. He cares so deeply for his people that He has given us clear guidelines on a subject that can overwhelm us if we try to tackle it alone. Like a parent who gives restrictions to children so they don't hurt themselves, God has told us clearly and without question that sexual immorality is nothing but trouble.

Sure, it may be enjoyable, but then sin is pleasant for a short time. But God looks at the big picture and sees the hurt, the pain, the tragedy that immorality brings. That's why He goes to great lengths in Scripture to tell us how to stay clean.

Enjoy baseball, basketball, and football. And sex. But remember, it's not a sport. There can be no road games.

DEBRIEFING

1. What is my biggest problem in regard to immoral sexual thoughts? How can I protect myself from those thoughts so they don't turn into wrong actions?

2. What, if anything, surprised me about the teaching in this devotional article?

3. How does what I read in 1 Corinthians 6:12–20 and 1 Thessalonians 4:3 give me a new appreciation for God and who he is?

CALL TO ACTION

1. I will pray each morning that God will protect me from these temptations, so they will never lead to sin:

    a. _____

    b. _____

    c. _____

2. To honor and respect my wife, and to enhance our own relationship, this week I will _____
_____.

Dear Father, thank you for your amazing plan of creation. You created sex and gave us clear guidelines so we won't get hurt because of it. Please help me to live within those guidelines every day out of love for you, to glorify you, and to let my wife know how special she is to me.

DATING YOUR WIFE

"A wife of noble character who can find? She is worth far more than rubies. Her husband has full confidence in her and lacks nothing of value" (Proverbs 31:10–11).

MARCHING ORDERS

FROM POINT MAN
Read: Chapter Three, page 58

FROM THE BIBLE
Read: Proverbs 31:10–31

Don't miss the significance of today's Scripture reading:

•When a man finds a wife of noble character, his life is, in one sense, complete.

•The characteristics of this kind of woman include concern for her husband and children, diligence, good business sense, a heart for the downcast, creativity, strength, dignity, and fear of God.

•The charm and beauty of youth are not as important as her character.

THINKING IT THROUGH

Crawl into the time machine with me.

Let's go back to those seemingly carefree days before you married the woman you call your wife.

Before the daily grind of the work world left you occasionally passing each other like commuters traveling opposite directions on the freeway.

Before the realities of living as "one" awakened each of you to the other's worst idiosyncrasies.

Before battles over the budget led to a war of words.

Before you discovered that she parks the car crooked in the garage, and she discovered that you never clean your shavings out of the sink in the morning.

Let's go back to the days when you couldn't wait to call her on the phone. When you planned for weeks to get her that special necklace, and then involved half the county in your elaborate plans to surprise her in the most romantic way. When you hated the night to end after a great date. When you didn't care if she had on grubby jeans, a sweatshirt, and a ball cap; she still looked like Miss Universe to you.

Let's go back to the days when you were still wooing her heart. Still winning her love. Still wondering and worrying if you were doing everything possible to show how much you cared. The days when you didn't know it, but you had already captured her heart and her only wish was that you would finally ask her to marry you.

Back in those days, you knew what you had. You had a girlfriend who was everything you ever wanted. She was Proverbs 31 personified — with youthful charm and beauty to go along with everything else. You had prayed and prayed for a woman like her, and God had again proved his graciousness.

Remember the feeling of holding her hand? Of walking along the lake? Of sitting across from her in a restaurant? Of taking long drives just to get away from the campus or her folks or your friends or the world?

Recall the little things you loved to do for her? The notes? The cards? The surprises? The kind words? The hugs?

Remember how her perfume smelled? How you stared at her picture whenever you were apart? How you would spend great amounts of time on the phone with her? How you'd drive hundreds of miles to see her? How every kiss was exciting?

Quite a ride in the time machine, wasn't it? But it is whirring to a halt, and it's time to step outside and get back to today.

To reality.

To the same woman. Yet now time has passed. Children have arrived. Troubles have occurred. Huge challenges have been tackled.

Life has taken on an urgency. In a rush, each day is lived on the edge. Time pressures you. Activities beckon you. Children depend on you. A job busies you. The church needs you. The world threatens you.

And your wife still loves you.

One of the tragic consequences of life's hectic pace is that husbands and wives can easily lose touch with one another. With those carefree days of dating a dim memory, and with the present pressures of real life bearing down on us from all sides, husbands and wives can easily neglect to find time for what got them together in the first place: pure and simple romance.

That's why it is so important for husbands and wives to date again. All too often, if they don't date each other, one of them will one day discover himself or herself dating someone else.

One of the best ways for a man to "rise up and call her blessed" is for him to make a mental return to their dating days. In other words, he needs to look for opportunities to bring back that same kind of romance into the marriage. What worked then should work now. After all, she's the same virtuous woman he married.

When we were in the time machine, we talked about some of the typical things a guy who is dating does for his best girl. Did those things mentioned sound familiar, and if not, did they recall for you some of the exciting things you used to do for your wife when you were on a mission to capture her heart?

Why not try some of them today? With the same fervor you had for her back then, begin to date your wife. Plan some surprises for her that will show her your love. Arrange for a baby-sitter if needed and take her to her favorite restaurant. Leave her some notes around the house. Order a bunch of her favorite flowers. Take her on a long walk. Go for a drive with the radio off.

Solomon asked, "A wife of noble character who can find?" Well, you did. And you won her heart once upon a time.

Can you win it again? Can you rebuild the heart-to-heart relationship you fought so hard to construct? Yes! And it could all begin today as you show her once more how special she is. Show her she's more worthy than ever of your attention.

MOTTO

Win your wife's heart all over again.

DEBRIEFING

1. When was the last time my wife and I had a date? Or is this something that we do quite often? What are some of the advantages I find in dating my wife?

2. As I look at Proverbs 31, I see many of my wife's traits. Which ones in particular should I tell her about?

3. How can I help my kids call their mother blessed?

CALL TO ACTION

1. In the next month, I will do the following things with my wife as dates:

a. _____

b. _____

c. _____

2. To help me recall the kinds of things we used to do together, I will talk with my wife about the things that made her happiest when we were dating.

Dear God, thank you for my wife. Thank you for her virtues, which first attracted me to her. Please help me to honor her still, in the midst of our busy lives, by spending time with her. Help us both to pay attention to each other in the same way we once did. Guide me as I try to show her my love.

RUN, DON'T WALK!

"He left his cloak in her hand and ran out of the house" (Genesis 39:12).

MARCHING ORDERS

FROM POINT MAN
Read: Chapter Three,
pages 60-71

FROM THE BIBLE
Read: Genesis 39

As you read today's Scripture passage, consider this:

•Because Joseph was a man of leadership, some would say he had a right to the spoils that came with the job.

•We all want to be noticed for our good looks and great physique, as Joseph was. But this kind of flattery did not go to his head.

•Joseph kept his cool in the face of sexual danger by focusing on the fact that there was a silent observer of the situation, and he didn't want to sin against him.

•Joseph ended up getting thrown in prison for his trouble. And he already had been sold into slavery. But God worked it out for good (Genesis 45:4-7).

THINKING IT THROUGH

There's a lot to admire about Joseph.

Who wouldn't want to be written up in Scripture as "well-built and handsome" (Genesis 39:6)? And to be honest, it must have been quite a compliment to be noticed by someone as important as the wife of the captain of the guard.

When we read Genesis 39:6, it's easy to be a bit jealous of Joseph and his physical attributes. Most of us go through life feeling rather poorly built, profoundly unhandsome, and little noticed.

But then it happens. You don't do anything to attract her attention, but suddenly a woman in the office or at church looks at you with a different kind of look. Not a you're-someone's-husband look, but a you're-interesting-to-me look.

That's always how it starts. A look. Then a return look. Followed by a word or two. And a longer conversation.

Suddenly a new feeling begins to overtake you. You feel well-built and handsome again. You begin to devise rationales for feeling this way. You look for new opportunities to talk with this woman. You think about her in your private moments. You stare at her when you think she's not looking.

If this happens — if you've entertained more than an initial tempting thought, you've gone too far. No, you haven't committed the acts of adultery, and it's not too late to cut out the monkey business. But if you didn't do what Joseph did, you have let the charade go too far.

Several things can happen when this kind of situation develops, and most of them are bad. Sometimes, the relationship stays in the non-physical realm, but if you let it continue even in that way, there's the danger of doing what Jesus told us not to do in the Sermon on the Mount: "I tell you that anyone who looks at a woman lustfully has already committed adultery with her in his heart" (Matthew 5:28). The goal is to flee before even this happens.

The most tragic result, of course, is to allow this new relationship to flourish and grow so out of control that it destroys a marriage.

The best result, no matter how far the temptation has taken

you, is still to run. Seek God's forgiveness for any wrongdoing, and immediately get out of the situation.

Joseph ran.

We need to run. Remember what 1 Corinthians 6 said? "Flee from sexual immorality." Like a rabbit hunter who scares up a bear, run! Don't think about it. Don't engage in conversation. Don't look back. Run!

It sounds so easy. Joseph took part in the original "Just Say No!" campaign. And it worked for him.

So why is it so hard to flee this temptation? Most often it has nothing to do with sex itself. Perhaps there is uneasiness at home; the husband and wife are at odds. Or maybe there is seeming incompatibility in other areas; the husband feels that his wife is not intellectually stimulating enough or that she isn't taking good enough care of herself. Or it could be that the normal pressures of raising children and making ends meet have left the couple too tired to enjoy each other's company as they did in the early years, so he is looking for tender companionship.

Once these rationales begin to take root in a man's thinking, he can easily begin to conclude that he deserves to have his intellectual or emotional or physical needs met by someone who seems more stimulating than his wife.

That kind of thinking is precisely why we are told to flee!

Don't take time to think it through, get moving!

Don't dwell on the possibilities, run!

Don't compare, hit the road!

One man who knew a lot about roads was Henry Ford, American entrepreneur and founder of the Ford Motor Company. He found success in the car industry by mass producing his Model T automobile. When he and his wife Clara reached their fiftieth wedding anniversary in 1938, Ford was asked the secret of his long marriage. He responded, "The formula is the same as I used to make a successful car. Stick to one model."

If we plan to stick to one model, then we have to flee all the others. We must run from any threat to sexual purity.

It's a fail-proof strategy for avoiding sexual sin. Yet that should be no surprise, because it comes directly from God himself. He knows us better than we do. He knows that the longer we dwell on bad thoughts, the better they start looking to us. He knows that the power of immoral sex can destroy us if we don't treat it like a mortal enemy.

Before Joseph ran from Potiphar's wife, we are told that "the Lord was with him." Later, after Joseph was thrown in jail based on her spurious testimony, we are again told, "the Lord was with him." Under God's blessing, Joseph was eventually elevated to the second highest post in the land and saved his family from certain doom.

Imagine the wreck of a life he would have lived had he not run from Potiphar's wife.

Like Joseph, let's not let anyone, however flirty, deter us from doing what is right.

MOTTO

Only a coward is afraid to run from sin.

DEBRIEFING

1. Is there a Potiphar's wife lurking out there in my life? What is the worst-case scenario in this situation? What do I need to do?

2. Besides specific women who might cause a problem, what other things do I need to flee to remain sexually pure?

3. How has God protected me from this temptation in the past? Have I thanked Him for it?

CALL TO ACTION

1. Each day before I head out into the world, I will remind myself: "Flee from sexual immorality" (1 Corinthians 6:18). How will I best remember to do that?

2. On the positive side, what three things will I do each day

to keep my attention focused more on my wife so that sexual temptation is less and less of a possibility?

Dear Lord, thank you for my wife. Please help me to pray for her each day and love her as I should. Give me courage to entertain no second thoughts or second looks at anyone who might cause me to stumble. Help me to flee temptation and to run toward you.

BEATITUDE LIVING

"Blessed are the poor in spirit, for theirs is the king-dom of heaven" (Matthew 5:3).

MARCHING ORDERS

FROM POINT MAN
Read: Chapter Three,
page 68

FROM THE BIBLE
Read: Matthew 5:1–10

In today's brief Bible reading, don't miss these points:

•Jesus took on a big task — telling us how to be happy.

• *Happy* as defined by these verses means "being blessed or congratulated by God." That's true happiness.

• Jesus talked about how we are to think and act, no matter what our circumstances.

THINKING IT THROUGH

What do you do when your circumstances have you imprisoned?

In *Point Man*, page 68, I refer to that kind of situation and mention that you could find yourself in a literal prison or in any number of confinements caused by such things as illness and marital problems.

And I mention that when circumstances take a direct hit on a marriage, the wrong response is to bail out and cause "the death of a small civilization," in Pat Conroy's words.

Yet, if you are in a situation like that, you probably are wondering, "Yeah, well, if my marital circumstances seem like a prison to me, then what am I supposed to do? Just grin and bear it?"

No, that's not a good final solution either. Neither giving up on the marriage or giving in to the circumstances is going to help. I'd like to suggest a third alternative.

Amid the circumstances you find yourself immersed in, try Beatitude Living.

This is an approach that means you take seriously the hard sayings of Jesus in Matthew 5. Known as the Beatitudes, the eight verses in Matthew 5:3–10 give us a pattern for thinking about life — a pattern that runs counter to how the world thinks but that results in our getting the congratulatory smile of God's approval on our life now and in heaven. Beatitude Living does not guarantee hassle-free circumstances, but it does promise a kind of divine happiness that no circumstances can offer.

Let's look at what Jesus said gives us God's nod of approval.

1. *Being poor in spirit* (verse 3). This does not refer to our financial condition; otherwise many of us would be on the right track without much effort. Instead, this refers to our attitude toward sin. We must admit our bankruptcy; we must see that we have nothing to offer God but our confession of sin. Only when we see our worthlessness without God's forgiveness can we receive the most important thing in our lives — God's gift of salvation.

2. *Being saddened by sin* (verse 4). Our society is making fun of sin at record rates these days. So much of what we see on TV or at the movies consists of people laughing at sin. What used to be unmentionable because it was wrong is now a laughing matter. Jesus takes a contrary view. He wants us to be saddened by sin. To find it disgusting. To see it as unwanted. God is pleased with us when we agree with Him that sin is reprehensible.

3. *Being meek* (verse 5). A quick clarification helps here. Jesus was meek. That should cancel any idea we had that meek equals

weak. Jesus was meek in that he withheld his power only for times when he needed it to protect God's holy name. He could have zapped the Roman soldiers who arrested him into next week, but he stood and allowed them to take him. After all, it was God's will for him to be taken. But when the money-changers in the temple offended his Father's house, he took decisive, powerful action. That's our model: Take action when God's will is under attack; show restraint when the affront is personal.

4. *Hungering and thirsting after righteousness* (verse 6). When you're hungry, you go after food aggressively and eagerly. When you're thirsty, nothing stops you from quenching that thirst. But tomorrow you'll be hungry and thirsty again. If we want righteousness in the same way, we'll pursue it and pursue it and pursue it again. We will fight for righteousness day after day after day. Not our rights, but righteousness according to God's Word. That kind of desire will help us stop focusing on our problems.

5. *Being merciful* (verse 7). When you are hurting, doesn't it feel good for someone to tell you he or she cares? Imagine how positive life could be for one with a merciful spirit. Not interested in number one, a merciful person seeks ways to relieve another's pain. In a marriage, a merciful person is invaluable and irresistible.

6. *Being pure in heart* (verse 8). I talk about adultery prevention in my *Point Man* chapter entitled "Real Men Don't," and think it's fair to say that if we can get a good handle on being pure in heart, we won't have a problem with adultery in a million years. A pure heart knows how to avoid circumstances, thoughts, actions, media offerings, photographs, and any other situations where impure thoughts can breed lust.

7. *Being a peacemaker* (verse 9). The only true peace that anyone can have is peace with God. Introducing someone to this peace is what Jesus is talking about. Secondarily, we are peacemakers when we cause the cessation of hostilities between believers. The ability to restore peace is an asset to any marriage.

8. *Being persecuted for righteousness* (verse 10). Often we think we are being persecuted when things go wrong, but Jesus was talking about persecution that comes because we have taken a stand for righteousness. Again, he emphasizes the importance of seeking righteousness, a quest every married couple should be on.

Prisoners of war often report that the only way they made it through the trauma of their confinement and torture was to keep their minds occupied with something more noble than what was happening to them. As Christians, we too can survive bad times if we keep our minds focused on the Lord. And one of the best ways to do that is through Beatitude Living.

MOTTO

Don't just love the Beatitudes, live them.

DEBRIEFING

1. Which of the Beatitudes are the most challenging to me?

2. If I were looking for God's congratulations in regard to the Beatitudes, for which of them would He congratulate me?

3. How can Beatitude Living help me in my circumstances?

CALL TO ACTION

1. What are the major problems I seem to be having in my marriage right now? Which Beatitudes will help me in my thinking?

2. What specific actions will I take to incorporate these three Beatitudes into my life?

a. "Blessed are those who mourn"

_____

b. "Blessed are the merciful"

_____

c. "Blessed are the pure in heart"

_____

Dear Lord, thank you for the Beatitudes and for the challenge they are to me. Please help me to rearrange my thinking to be a Beatitude person. Help me to overcome bad circumstances through right thinking. Thank you for the peace I have with you through Jesus, and help me to show God's peace to others.

LOOKING FOR MAJOR LEAGUE FORGIVENESS

*"I said, 'I will confess my transgressions to the Lord'
and you forgave the guilt of my sin" (Psalm 32:5).*

MARCHING ORDERS

FROM POINT MAN
**Read: Chapter Three,
pages 71-79**

FROM THE BIBLE
Read: Psalm 32

Don't miss the significance of today's Scripture reading:

• Psalm 32 is David's call for forgiveness, which he sorely needed after his escapades in the Bathsheba affair.

• David, who committed huge sins in that situation with Bathsheba, sounds like a happy person in this Psalm.

• Clearly, David spent some time refusing to confess. Notice how he described that time (verses 3–4).

• David ends the psalm on an upbeat, positive note. Think of how that corresponds with what he had done and what he needed from God.

THINKING IT THROUGH

It's hard for us to forgive.

We want justice done. We want things made right. We wish the worst for the wrongdoer because we know what grief he or she has caused others.

We look at what David did in 2 Samuel 11 and are shocked. Adultery. Deceit. Murder.

It's the stuff of made-for-TV movies that we don't let our kids see and shouldn't watch ourselves.

It's families destroyed and a kingdom embarrassed because of one man's lack of self-control. It's tabloid news that we leave on the rack at the grocery store.

If we were around in David's time, how could we forgive him?

How could we overlook his ruthless treatment of a loyal soldier like Uriah? And for him to end up married to Bathsheba after misusing her so blatantly would be too much for us to stomach.

We would look back in Samuel's record and see that in his first scroll, God had called David, "a man after His own heart" (1 Samuel 13:14). "How could that be?" we would sniff, knowing that we could never do the evil deeds David did.

Yes, forgiveness is tough work for us.

But it is exactly what most of us need. And it's a good thing it's not up to us in our human frailty to grant it where it deserves to be given.

Let's look honestly at ourselves. We've been reading over the past few days about sexual sins. David committed the ultimate sexual sin.

Yet we all must admit that even if we haven't fallen to the depths David did, we've at least fallen to some degree. Whether it was a lustful look; an inappropriate comment; a sneaking, voyeuristic glance at a media presentation of sex; or some other indiscretion, we need forgiveness.

But maybe you have gone beyond that.

Perhaps you too have fallen as far as David did. In a weak moment, you allowed the enemy to convince you that you deserved something new, fresh, and exciting. Now you feel dirty and dulled by the experience. You can't face your wife anymore with the same vibrancy you once felt. You can't communicate directly with God either, for the lines of communication have somehow been shut off. Worship is a charade, and life is a chore. The thrill of the conquest has left you feeling the pressure of the hunted, because being found out is your worst fear and your most constant thought.

You've done what David did; you need to follow through as he did.

Let's look at the progression.

As you begin to read Psalm 32, you can sense the joy, the cleansing, the absolute ecstasy that David discovered in God's forgiveness. He is a man who is blessed. He is a man who realizes that in God's remarkable grace is found exoneration. David the guilty can return to being David the guilt-free. He knows that God is not counting his sin against him anymore.

Yet when you get to verse 3, you discover that it took a while for David to get to the place where he could find forgiveness.

Like all of us, he tried to live with his sin. He "kept silent." He thought he could handle the guilt by himself, without God's assistance. But the longer he did that, the worse things got.

Sadness was his constant companion. It's always that way when we seek pleasure through ungodly means. The temporary thrill quickly turns into a malaise that won't disappear. David described it as "groaning all day long."

Remember the last time you had the flu? Does "groaning all day long" sound familiar? In a spiritual sense, when we are sick with sin, our spiritual body aches and we are incapacitated.

David felt the hand of God on him because of his sin (verse 4), making the weight of his sin unbearable. He couldn't stand up under it because his spiritual strength was depleted — just like our physical strength is wiped out under the blazing sun of a 100-degree day.

Does any of this sound familiar? Perhaps the sin is not sexual, but some other violation of God's clear teaching.

If these are your symptoms, don't delay the cure. David finally wised up to the solution. "Then I acknowledged my sin to You," he writes, "and did not cover up my iniquity. I said, 'I will confess my transgressions to the Lord' — and You forgave the guilt of my sin" (verse 5).

Only at that point could David begin to feel the oppression lift and the guilt be swept away. Only then could he again enjoy fellowship with God and find life worth living again.

Forgiveness. It's one of God's great gifts to us. Use it to its fullest. Let its joy refill your heart and reenergize your life.

MOTTO

Instead of staggering under the weight of sin, let
Jesus lift you up with his forgiveness.

DEBRIEFING

1. When was the last time I experienced God's forgiveness? How did it make me feel?

2. Can I say, as David did, "Rejoice in the Lord and be glad"? Or am I feeling the weight of unforgiven sin?

3. Even though I might be forgiven by God, what might be some consequences of sin that even God's forgiveness won't nullify?

CALL TO ACTION

The next time I stumble into wrong action that I know violates God's clear commands, I will take the following steps:

1. Confess my sin to God and agree with Him about it (1 John 1:9).

2. Make any needed restitution.

3. Praise God for His forgiveness and restoration.

Dear gracious Father, thank you for providing a way for me to be for-given. You offered forgiveness through the death, burial, and resurrection, giving me freedom from the ultimate penalty of my sin. You also offered to keep fellowship with me open by forgiving my sins while I'm still here on this earth. Please help me to refrain from sin, and thank you for your forgiveness.

HEADED FOR LEADERSHIP?

"And the things you have heard me say in the presence of many witnesses entrust to reliable men who will also be qualified to teach others" (2 Timothy 2:2).

As you read today's Scripture passage, consider this:

• According to verse 7, the right kind of leaders are those who speak the Word of God and have lives worth imitating.

• In verse 17, we find out how we are to respond to those God has put into leadership positions.

THINKING IT THROUGH

How would you like to be President of the United States?

It's an incredibly scary thought, isn't it? To have to try to be the leader of 275,000,000 people. To make decisions every day that affect millions of people. To try to bring into focus a strategy for an entire country. To know that no matter how hard you try or what you do, a significant portion of people will not like what you do.

If that prospect seems too daunting, then how about something a bit less imposing, but maybe more important?

How would you like to be a leader in the church?

Now, perhaps more than at any time in church history, we need leadership. We've seen leaders fall to the wayside because of sin, and they must be replaced. Also, with a growing trend toward the secularization of society in general and of the church in particular, Christians with leadership potential are not as plentiful as perhaps they should be.

The New Testament shows us how leadership can be taught and what kind of people become leaders.

Consider, for instance, the disciples. These were ordinary men of apparently limited leadership potential. From fishermen to tax collectors, the men Jesus Christ called to be his special group of followers had never shown signs of being in-charge people before Jesus took them under his wing.

Jesus, however, taught them carefully and diligently, making sure they learned everything they would need to know.

And consider what their mission was. After Jesus went back to heaven, he left the propagation of the world's most important message in their hands. Had they not been effective in relaying the gospel of Jesus Christ, what would have happened? Christianity would have died.

From the experience of the disciples under Jesus' tutelage, we see three factors about leadership:

• Godly leaders need training.

• Godly leaders need a mission.

• Godly leaders can be trusted.

Do you feel the call of God to be a leader? Or have you already been a leader for quite some time? In either case, if you have any designs on assuming a leadership role in the church, perhaps it's time to reexamine your effectiveness according to these three guidelines.

Training. Whether you are a deacon, a teacher, a Bible study leader, or the church treasurer, you need to continually upgrade your knowledge of God's Word.

Mission. Jesus himself gave us two great missions. He said we should win others to Christ, and he said we should love our neighbors as ourselves. Beyond those parts of our mission, we also know we need to take care of our family and provide for them.

Perhaps it would be helpful to draft a mission statement for your leadership role — a document that you can return to time and again to measure your leadership effectiveness.

Trustworthiness. According to Hebrews 13:7, it is expected of leaders that they will live in a way that others can follow them. In a sense, leaders have a bigger responsibility to be morally strong because their fall would affect many. In areas of honesty, morality, and the tongue, leaders must make extra care to be godly.

Let's say you don't find yourself drawn to church leadership. You've examined your spiritual gifts and honestly discovered that you are out of place trying to take on a leadership role in the body of Christ. After all, if there are no followers, who's there to lead?

If this is where you find yourself, you still cannot be excused from leadership roles. Right there in your home is a group of people who need your guidance. All too often, we men fail to lead where we are most needed — behind our own front door.

This is a role none of us can afford to skip. When we have a family, we are all destined for leadership. It may not be a leadership role with the glamour of the presidency or the responsibility of working in the church, but it is perhaps the most essential leadership role in society.

At home, we have to be the school principal, the pastor, and the Sunday school superintendent all wrapped up in one. We will make major decisions, with the help of our wives, on dozens of matters each week. And these decisions will have far-reaching effects on our family.

Leadership. It's a great challenge that takes training, a sense of mission, and trustworthiness. Whether we are the president of the United States or the head of a family, it's a role we cannot neglect.

*As the head of a family, we can't afford to follow or
get out of the way; we must lead.*

1. What kind of leadership roles do I enjoy?

2. What kind of leadership roles do I despise?

3. What training have I had to be a good dad? What more do I need?

CALL TO ACTION

1. To get a handle on the big picture, I will look for and find at least one book on leadership and read it.

2. If I were to evaluate my own leadership effectiveness in the following areas, what grade would I give myself?

    a. vision

    b. implementation of ideas

    c. delegating

    d. working with people

    e. problem solving

Dear Lord, please help me to be the leader in my home that I need to be, and guide me as I pursue other leadership opportunities. Help me know how to incorporate your principles in my leadership. Show me how Jesus led and what I can learn from Him.

ONE IS THE ONLY NUMBER

"Now the overseer must be above reproach, the husband of but one wife..." (1 Timothy 3:2).

MARCHING ORDERS

FROM POINT MAN
Read: Chapter Four,
pages 81-89

FROM THE BIBLE
Read: I Timothy 3:1–7

In today's brief Bible reading, don't miss these points:

•These guidelines for church leaders contain some rather stiff requirements, not the least of them being the one-man, one-woman concept of marriage.

•The passage contains other family values statements too. Notice that they deal with the matter of how a man should lead his family.

THINKING IT THROUGH

Some people would call the message of 1 Timothy 3:2 "pie in the sky."

To think that a man and a woman who are in their early twenties could pair up with each other and commit the rest of their lives to each other! "Ridiculous," many say. "Can't be done. You might as well sentence a man to life in prison without the possibility of parole."

Yet it happens. It can be done!

And it is required for some leadership positions in the church.

Let me break in for just a moment and say a word to you if you find yourself unable to meet this qualification. At one time, you thought you were in a marriage for the long haul, but then something horrible happened. Before your eyes, and before you could do anything about it, your marriage disintegrated.

Your dream of a one-woman lifetime became the nightmare of divorce.

Frankly, unless that original partnership can be reconciled, there isn't anything you can do about it now. You have probably already sought spiritual counsel. If the sin is yours, make sure you've taken the route of David in Psalm 32. And if you were wronged, check yourself to see if you've learned the difficult art of forgiving.

You are now on the other side of it, and in effect, you are looking at marriage again with the same hopes you looked at it the first time. If so, then these words still have meaning to you.

For every man currently in a marriage, the goal is still the same. Because God hates divorce and because he despises sexual sin, your task is to be a one-woman man.

Those who say this is "pie-in-the-sky" ignore human experience and doubt God's power. We know it can happen. My parents, James and Beverly Farrar, have done it. My wife, Mary, and I are committed to making it happen.

God calls each of us to be a one-woman man. We must either trust the Designer that His plan works, or forget the whole thing. If the Designer is to be trusted, then it is essential to read His instructions.

1. *Nurture the relationship.* In Deuteronomy 24 we see a rather startling example of the importance of a husband building the relationship with his wife. "If a man has recently married," Deuteronomy 24:5 says, " he must not be sent to war or have any other duty laid on him. For one year he is to be free to stay at

home and bring happiness to the wife he has married."

This is not a New Testament principle, so don't call your employer and tell him or her that you deserve a retroactive year off for a belated honeymoon. Yet it illustrates the value of nurturing the husband-wife bond early in a marriage. And that can be done only when ample time is spent together. A one-woman man carves out special times to be with his wife to show her how special she is to him.

2. *See her as a blessing.* Too often we look at a wife's faults and dwell on the trouble she causes. How counterproductive! Proverbs 18:22 shows that a wife is a gift from God and should be cherished. Seeing her as a special delivery direct from God changes our perception of her. It sets her up as a person who will enhance our life because of her God-given abilities. A one-woman man sees his wife as a tremendous blessing from God, and treats her with the respect she deserves.

3. *Love her unabashedly.* Did you ever think it strange that in Ephesians 5:33, Paul has to tell men something so obvious? He says, "each one of you must love his wife as he loves himself." It's like telling a guy with a brand-new Jeep Grand Cherokee, "You must love your new vehicle."

Yet, Paul knew what he was doing. We men need a push sometimes to love our wives as we should. So let me suggest that you show your wife some no-holds-barred, forget-the-embarrassment, you're-really-special love. I'm not talking about making love here. That's too easy.

I'm talking about saying nice things to your colleagues about her. About putting your arm around her in public. About stopping right now and saying, "Hey, Honey! Thanks for being my wife. I love you!" (If she needs smelling salts, you get them. Don't ask her to.)

A one-woman man loves his wife unashamedly, unabashedly, and undeniably. And she knows it.

The scriptural call for a man to have one wife is not a call to an impossible ideal. It is a call to a reachable goal, one that is highly dependent on the husband's willingness to love his wife as he should. Marriage for a lifetime, which is God's design, can be your reality. And your true, genuine love, will make it a great adventure.

MOTTO

To be a one-woman man takes dedication to God's marital plan.

DEBRIEFING

1. As I think back over how I have treated my wife in the past week, how would I characterize my interaction with her? What about it makes me happy, and what makes me sad?

2. In Ephesians 5:22–33, what principles of marriage can I find that will help me be more loving?

3. How long has it been since I looked back at my wedding vows to see what I actually committed to that day? How often should I review those vows?

CALL TO ACTION

1. Which of these sentences does my wife need to hear me say more often?

   a. You are beautiful.

   b. I love you.

   c. Thanks for being my wife.

   d. You are my best friend.

   e. What can I do for you?

   f. Let's talk.

2. How often have I told my wife (since our wedding) that I love her and plan to spend the rest of my life with her? When can I tell her again?

Dear God, thank you for my wife. She is the perfect complement in my life. Thank you that she helps me_____.
Please show me how to love her more deeply. Help me to honor you by honoring her each day in a new, fresh way.

IN IT FOR THE LONG RUN

"Let us run with perseverance the race marked out for us"
(Hebrews 12:1).

MARCHING ORDERS

FROM POINT MAN
Read: Chapter Four,
pages 86-88

FROM THE BIBLE
Read: Hebrews
12:1–11

Don't miss the significance of today's Bible reading:

• Whatever it means to be "surrounded by such a great cloud of witnesses," we know that our life's pathway is being observed.

• The worst hindrance to our staying with our task is not difficulties or obstacles but sin.

• We have a definite pathway "marked out for us," and it is our job to complete that course.

THINKING IT THROUGH

We all know about Cal Ripken Jr. and his remarkable string of consecutive baseball games. NBA fans recognize the name of A.C. Green as the active player with the longest run of games played without missing one, and they know that he is third all-time on the ironman list.

But have you ever heard of Frances Cameron? What she did makes both Ripken's and Green's records pale in comparison, simply because what she did has eternal significance. She's not a shortstop or a power forward; she's a Sunday school teacher. And her consecutive class record spans seventy-two years. She's been studying her lesson and presenting God's Word to her students ever since Herbert Hoover was President, before Babe Ruth hit sixty home runs, and before there was television, modern Israel, the United Nations, and night baseball.

These are three examples of people in it for the long run. They are not going to let any kind of hindrance stand between them and what they feel is their appointed task.

According to the author of Hebrews, we all have an appointed task, and our job is to stick to it with perseverance. That task might be the specific ministry God has called us to — like Frances Cameron and her Sunday school classes. It might be the occupation God has directed us to use for his glory — like A.C. Green, a Christian who is using his platform as a basketball player to further the gospel.

And that job might be marriage, if God has put us in that situation. That is definitely a "race marked out for us." If we want to accomplish it successfully, that means staying in it for the long run.

When Cal Ripken began his streak, he didn't know he would stand in the glory of a nation's adulation thirteen years later. He had no way of foreseeing that incredible victory lap around Camden Yards to honor one of the most remarkable achievements in sports history. All he knew was that his job was to play hard every day, take care of his body, and not do anything stupid that would cause injury. He had a regimen, a dedication, and a love for the game. He had what it takes to persevere.

So do you. As you look at your marriage, no matter what stage of it you are in — whether you are a newlywed in a first marriage, a marriage veteran who is eager to make a second marriage work, or an "old-timer" with a couple of decades or more in the bank — you have resources that can help you stick to the task for the long haul.

In Hebrews 12, we see what some of the resources and training rules are. These apply to the Christian life and to marriage — and anything else God calls you to do.

•Significant others are watching you, hoping for your success (verse 1).

•Hindrances can be cast aside, making the race easier (verse 1). We know from reading Matthew 11:28–30 that Jesus will take our burdens; we see in Galatians 6:2 that we can share our burdens with other believers.

•Sin is a weight that slows down our pursuit of our goal of perseverance. In a marriage, sexual sin, dishonesty, deceit, greed, pride, and an uncontrolled tongue are all sins that we must avoid if we want to stay in it for the long term.

•Like an athlete who fixes his thoughts on the championship and then lets nothing distract him or her from doing what it takes to achieve it, we must keep focused on Jesus. Concentrating on his perseverance will help us to avoid being sidetracked by our own difficulties. We know what he suffered on our behalf, so we can endure the tough times in our lives for him.

There's an added dimension to this idea of perseverance, but it is not one we are particularly fond of. Along life's road, if we happen to fail in our attempts to avoid sin, we may face God's discipline. When we do, however, God is demonstrating His fatherly love for us. As a result of God's discipline, we will later enjoy "righteousness and peace" (verse 11). But if we allow the discipline to turn us away from God like a rebellious child turns from a parent, we will neither persevere nor enjoy God's blessings.

Did you ever play a sport? As you played, weren't there times when you wanted to walk up to the coach, fling your uniform at his feet, and tell him you had enough with the push ups, the laps, the lectures, the criticism, and the pressure? And weren't there times when the coach's constant correction of your errors made you want to hang it up?

But if you didn't, and if you stuck with it, can you recall the thrill of completing a season, earning your letter, or perhaps winning a championship?

In marriage, the road sometimes seems too long. The bumps seem too jarring. The detours seem to slow things down too much. The construction seems never-ending. But this is the pathway God has marked out for you. And He has given you everything you need to persevere.

Stick with it. You may not be rewarded with a standing ovation by 50,000 people, but you will get God's approval. And you'll enjoy the satisfaction that comes from sticking with it for the long run.

MOTTO

The road may be long, but the destination is worth the trip.

DEBRIEFING

1. How do I view my marriage: a lifetime commitment, a here-and-now situation, or a convenient relationship? How does my wife view it? How does God?

2. Who are some people I admire because they have proved their perseverance in the path marked out for them?

3. In what ways has God equipped me to make my marriage work for the long term? What obstacles do I have to overcome?

CALL TO ACTION

1. What positive steps will I take to enhance my relationship with my wife and make her feel secure in our relationship?

2. The following hindrances could hold me back in pursuing marriage as a life-time commitment. What will I do with each hindrance?

Hindrance	Action
_____	_____
_____	_____
_____	_____
_____	_____
_____	_____
_____	_____
_____	_____

Dear God, thank you for my marriage. Please help me to prepare daily to be the husband I should be. Help eliminate the sins that can trip me up, and help me negotiate the obstacles that slow me down. Show me how to have the commitment I need. Thank you for your guidance, wisdom, and grace.

PRETTY WOMAN

"You are beautiful, my darling..." (Song of Solomon 6:4).

MARCHING ORDERS

FROM POINT MAN
Read: Chapter Four,
pages 88-89

FROM THE BIBLE
Read: Genesis
12:10-20

As you read today's Scripture passage, consider this:

•When Abram and Sarai went to Egypt, Sarai was no high school cheerleader. Abram was past more than seventy-five years old, and she was only a decade behind.

•Abram was right in his estimation of Sarai's beauty, for the Egyptian officials were impressed when they saw her.

•Later, Sarai bears Isaac when she is not too many years shy of 100.

THINKING IT THROUGH

Let's face it. Some women are prettier than others. It doesn't take a beauty contest judge to figure that out.

Yet there are also matters of taste that figure in to this question of beauty. One man finds a certain woman attractive even though he may have a friend who doesn't see her beauty the same way. It's a good thing it works out this way, since there is such a variety of beauty in the world.

The woman you chose to be your wife — that woman who attracted your attention with her beauty, her charm, her intelligence, and maybe even her ability to bake a mean German chocolate cake — must be to you the most beautiful woman in the world.

You must be able to say to her as the writer of the Song of Solomon said, "You are beautiful, my darling."

It must be a heartfelt expression. The pretty woman who shares your bed must be to you the epitome of loveliness.

And wherever you go with your bride, you should be able to look in her face, as Abram did to his well-along-in-years wife Sarai, and say, "I know what a beautiful woman you are." Even if she's as old as Phyliss Diller.

This activity should be daily, yet never routine. Every day, the woman you married must hear from your lips how beautiful she is. Every day, you must be able to thank God for her and praise his guidance that led the two of you together.

Some men, though, as the marriage travels along its inevitable pathway, lose sight of the beauty of their wives. They usually do so in three ways.

• *Their wandering eyes begin to land on other pretty women.* Comparison shopping is a great idea when you're looking for a new power saw, but when it happens in a marriage, it's always a bad deal.

• *They leave God and his sovereignty out of the equation.* Once you stop depending on the fact that God led you together, you begin to imagine you could be happier with someone younger and more beautiful. (Remember, if you continue to consider your wife the most beautiful woman alive, this will not be a problem.)

• *They dwell on the wrong kind of beauty.* A woman who dedicates herself to taking care of her family at all costs, who goes out of the way to care for her husband as his complement, and who takes on other activities that help the family can grow tired. She can lose that youthful glow and freshness that attracted her husband when they were both scrubbed-up young people. Yet in doing those activities, she will develop a deeper, more important beauty. To ignore that beauty is a disservice to the woman who gave her youthful years to you.

If a man wants to avoid dwelling on what he perceives to be the negative factors of aging (remember Abram called his wife beautiful well past age seventy-five, and he fathered a child with her when she was ninety), there are some positive steps he can take.

• *Do the Abram thing.* Never let a day go by without snuggling up to your wife and whispering in her ear how beautiful she is.

• *Involve God.* Thank Him for your wife.

• *Make her feel special.* A lot of times a wife can let herself go in the looks department if her special man does not give her reason to fight the battle. By giving her time off from the rat race, by getting her some clothes that make her feel pretty, by taking her out on the town occasionally, by treating her with respect in public, by bragging about her to others, by taking her away for a romantic weekend, and by giving her a break with the kids, you can give her incentive to make sure she looks nice for you.

If you treat her like Cinderella and never let her go to the ball, she'll never get a chance to show you what a beautiful woman she is.

God's design for humans is clearly different from the design we would have put together. He made humans to have their greatest physical beauty at the young child-bearing age, for that helps the attraction that leads to the propagation of the race. We, however, would love to see that teenage and early marriage beauty last an entire life.

Yet if it did, we might miss out on the secondary beauty that comes through maturity. That beauty is what we need to dwell on as the twenties become thirties, the thirties become forties, and as middle age gives way to old age. It's a beauty that is nurtured by long walks on an autumn evening or special lunch-time get-togethers. It comes from the satisfaction of having raised a family or having persevered the financial tough times together. It comes from the security of knowing that regardless of the situation, those vows of marriage made so long ago are still good — even if poorer days outnumber richer ones or if sickness is more prevalent than health.

Abram looked at barren, elderly Sarai and saw nothing but beauty.

Is that the way you feel about the pretty woman God gave you?

DEBRIEFING

1. In the past week, how often have I told my wife how beautiful she is? Is that enough?

2. What other statements do I use to make her feel special? Do I tell her she looks nice in a new dress? Do I tell her I can't believe she looks so great after such a tough day? Do I tell her that I can't wait to be alone with her at night?

3. What have I done recently that might make me be more inclined toward some other pretty women? What should I do about that?

CALL TO ACTION

1. In the next week, I will leave five notes, phone messages, e-mail comments, greeting cards, or other missives telling my wife how beautiful she is.

2. Today or tomorrow I will look for several ways I can compliment my wife on one of the special things she does for our family so I can commend her inner beauty.

3. Within the next three months, I will plan one weekend getaway during which I will spend my entire time romancing her.

Dear Lord, thank you for my beautiful wife. Thank you for leading us together. Please keep my attention on her alone. Clear my mind of distractions. When I need to be awakened to the beauty that goes beneath the surface, help me notice it and tell her about it.

EYE SURGERY

"If your right eye causes you to sin, gouge it out..."
(Matthew 5:29).

FROM POINT MAN
Read: Chapter Four,
pages 89-97

FROM THE BIBLE
Read: Matthew
5:27–30

As you read today's Scripture, think about these questions:

•Jesus' first comment in this passage is a verification of a teaching that had been passed down for generations — since Moses received the Ten Commandments. Now, though, he seems to be making sexual restrictions even more tight. Could it be that the one who knows our inmost thoughts wanted to warn us how damaging wrong thoughts could be?

•Generally, Jesus' words are to be taken literally. How do you respond to such a statement as, "If your right eye causes you to sin, gouge it out"?

THINKING IT THROUGH

To be brutally honest, sometimes you just can't help but notice.

Girls. Females. Women.

I think we'd be better off with a little more of the Middle East cover-everything-but-the-eyes mentality in this country than our show-everything-but-the-essentials way of thinking. It is difficult for a guy who desires to remain pure-minded to walk the mall or visit an amusement park or go to a ball game without noticing some inviting scenery.

Do you ever wonder how some mothers can possibly let their daughters out of the house looking the way they do? But then you see the mothers (actually more of them than you wanted to) and you get the connection.

So what are we to do? We can't be gouging out our eyes every time some well-endowed female walks by in a halter top.

First, *start with a clean slate.* When you read Jesus' shocking words, "anyone who looks at a woman lustfully has already committed adultery in his heart" (Matthew 5:28), it probably goes without saying that unless you lead an incredibly sheltered life, it has happened. If so, stop right now and confess those lustful looks to God and ask His forgiveness.

Second, *make a concentrated effort to avoid those situations that would tempt you to further lustful thinking.* Skip the movies where female bodies are paraded for your viewing pleasure. Ask your wife to dispose of that annual sports magazine that shows more skin than sports. And in those public places where undiscerning females uncover too much, ask for eye protection from God.

Third, *continue to nurture your relationship with your wife,* and as the song says, have eyes only for her.

Besides those three guiding concepts, Solomon also has some great suggestions for avoiding trouble with women. To make sure you never need the eye surgery Jesus talked about in Matthew 5, consider Solomon's father-to-son warnings about the wiles of women found in Proverbs 6:20–29.

1. *Keep right teaching in mind as you make your way through life* (verses 20–22). Lustful thoughts are most problematic when we let them push aside standards that we know are true. Each time we view a sexually lust-filled scene in a video or on TV, for example, we must first convince ourselves that we can set aside God's standards to do so. Whether those standards are from our "father's

commands," our "mother's teaching," or our own study of the Word, they guide us until we consciously block them out.

2. *Notice the contrast between the light of right teaching and the immorality of the woman who would seduce you* (verses 23–24). Also, notice the contrast between discipline and the waywardness of the seductive woman. Clearly, sexual sin, which the world depicts as so carefree and joyous, leads to everything that a godly man should abhor.

3. *Never forget that succumbing to the lust of beauty and being seduced by tempting eyes are demeaning to the believer* (verses 25–26). Can there be a better picture of the degradation of sexual sin than this: "the prostitute reduces you to a loaf of bread" (Proverbs 6:26)? Don't let yourself be brought to such a low level.

4. *Don't play with fire* (verses 27–29). For thousands of years, men have tried to get away with sexual sin. They never, ever do. Oh, they may think no one knows, but the consequences of their actions always come to light. The best way to avoid this awful legacy is to keep the blinders on your eyes and keep them home.

Professional athletes are notoriously bad at this. They have developed a reputation as womanizers always on the prowl. Making things easy for them is a constant influx of new women who would love to fulfill their desires. They would do anything to be connected sexually with these men of power, money, and fame.

Not all athletes, though, succumb to the threats. One who avoids the heartache and embarrassment of sexual sin is Mark Price, who played for many years with the Cleveland Cavaliers before moving on to the Washington Bullets. He has a great routine for protecting himself against the flirtations of women who would turn him into a loaf of bread.

After anything happens with a woman who shows any improper interest in him while Mark is away from home, Mark goes back to his hotel room, calls his wife Laura, and he tells her what happened. This open line of communication allows him to be honest with her about the sexual threats, and they end, he says, usually having a laugh over it.

Price, a strong Christian, follows the biblical guidelines, and it is saving him and his family untold trouble. He has eyes only for Laura.

And Jesus.

In Hebrews 12:2, the writer says, "Let us fix our eyes on Jesus, the author and perfecter of our faith." When we keep our focus on him, it makes it very tough to refocus on those women whose beauty might send our thought patterns down the wrong paths.

Keep looking at Jesus. Keep nurturing your relationship with your wife. Doing those two things is a lot easier than undergoing radical eye surgery.

MOTTO

Looking at Jesus and your wife gives you little time to look elsewhere.

DEBRIEFING

1. I know when I have gone beyond glancing and started lusting. What signal can I give myself to avoid doing that?

2. Is my relationship with my wife strong enough that I can talk to her about this problem?

3. What would help me keep my focus more on Jesus, which would guide me to right thinking in the middle of a society that places a lot of temptation in front of my eyes?

CALL TO ACTION

1. What are three programs or movies I watched in the past week that I should have turned off or walked out on?

2. The next time I find my eyes wandering, I will remember these three reasons for keeping my vision on Jesus:

a. _____

b. _____

c. _____

Dear Heavenly Father, thank you for my wife. Please help me to appreciate her beauty. Keep me from looking wrongfully at other women, and strengthen me to keep my eyes on Jesus.

STRAP IT ON

"Put on the full armor of God so that you can take your stand against the devil's schemes" (Ephesians 6:11).

MARCHING ORDERS

FROM POINT MAN
Read: Chapter Four,
pages 97-107

FROM THE BIBLE
Read: Ephesians
6:10–18

In today's brief Bible passage, don't miss these points:

• A strong battle is brewing in our lives. We have to be on guard against the devil's plans, against the powers of this dark world, and against evil spiritual forces. It may sound like a Peretti novel, but this is the real thing.

• A wide-ranging array of equipment has been set out for us — equipment that is especially suited for the battles we face. Our job is to put it on and pray.

THINKING IT THROUGH

No matter how much talent Troy Aikman, Steve Young, or Joe Montana possess as football players, they would be absolutely no good to their teams without protection.

Suppose the Cowboys were going up against the Steelers, and they inserted an offensive line consisting of 170-pound point guards. Then they sent Aikman behind center wearing his street clothes and a nifty 'Boys baseball cap. Well, despite Aikman's considerable ability, the man would be run over like a possum on the freeway. The Steelers would be all over him before he could find the laces on the ball.

Without protection, a football player is helpless.

The protection he gets from the equipment he wears and the protection he receives from his teammates are absolutely essential to his success.

Same goes for us.

We can have a pretty good record as Christians, but if we try to go up against our opponent all alone and unprotected, we're an easy mark for Satan. He'll run us down so fast we won't have time to get his license plate number.

In the battle we've been talking about — the battle to keep ourselves sexually pure and to avoid the traps of temptation — we can't afford to go unprotected. The devil has more schemes than a Hall of Fame coach, and he has more power than the fiercest front line. To attempt to battle him in our spiritual street clothes would be like sending in your kid's junior high team against the Chicago Bears.

The promise in Ephesians 6 is pretty remarkable. It clearly reminds us we can have confidence against the enemy if we dress for success.

So, let's head to the equipment room of Ephesians 6 and see what gear God has for us there to strap on.

Belt of Truth (verse 14). Have you ever noticed how many times Jesus said, "I tell you the truth" when he was on earth? In the gospels, that phrase appears dozens of times. Perhaps it is no surprise that the One who called Himself "the way, the truth, and the life" (John 14:6) constantly reminded His listeners of the importance of saying what is true.

And it is no surprise that those who reject the truth are headed for the bad side of God's plan. Romans 2:8 says, "But for those who are self-seeking and who reject the truth and follow evil, there will be wrath and anger." Think about your sexuality and this verse. Think of all the opportunities to reject the truth of Scripture about morality and do wrong. Either we wear that belt of truth around our waist and control our sexual tendencies or we "reject the truth" and reap the wrath and anger of God's punishment.

I don't know about you, but the contrast makes me want to strap on that belt of truth and keep it on.

Breastplate of Righteousness (verse 14). Are you familiar with Steve Green's song, "Guard Your Heart"? I can't think of a better picture for us of what a breastplate of righteousness can do for us. It protects the innermost thought processes of our being by keeping from us the evil that would enjoy getting its stranglehold on us.

Righteousness is something to live for. And something Jesus died for, according to 1 Peter 2:24. Because of Jesus' sacrifice, we can die to sins and live for righteousness.

Living for righteousness means filtering all decisions through our biblical grid, making sure our actions and words are pleasing to the Lord. That's how we guard our heart against any threats to our marriage.

Strap on the breastplate of righteousness and watch the devil's darts bounce right off.

Boots of the Gospel (verse 15). It is amazing how many Christian marriages get derailed. Something goes wrong between two of God's children, and another train wreck occurs.

Somehow, the gospel has been unloosed from the feet of those folks, and they begin to stumble around in their own self-styled philosophy.

When we place our feet in the boots of the gospel, we're able to remain on the right path. The gospel teaches us the submission necessary for a marriage to survive, for Jesus Christ submitted himself to God's will for his death and resurrection. By the same token, Christ's death teaches us the selfless service of sacrifice. The gospel also teaches us to forgive just as we are forgiven. It teaches us to love unconditionally, as the Savior loves us. Those lessons straight from the gospel will direct our feet, enabling us to walk by the Spirit — if we keep our boots on.

Shield of Faith (verse 16). How much faith do you have in God? Do you have faith to believe that He guided you to your marriage partner?

If we hold the shield of faith in God and His sovereignty out in front of us, we'll be protected from the doubts, justifications, rationalizations, and other fiery arrows that can turn us away from our spouse.

Strap on the shield of faith as a reminder that God is trustworthy, and what He does for us is good and right.

Helmet of Salvation (verse 17). If you guard your heart and let the enemy start working on your head, you still may lose the war. To avoid that, "conduct yourselves in a manner worthy of the gospel of Christ" (Philippians 1:27). When our minds are centered on Christ and what he did on the cross, we are protected from all kinds of attacks.

Sword of the Spirit (verse 17). Fighting off the onslaughts of Satan is not a one-man show. We need big-time help. And that help comes in the person of the Holy Spirit. He alone can empower us to use our knowledge of the gospel and other gear to stop the enemy. When our weakness is at its peak, the Holy Spirit flashes the sword of his power to keep us safe.

That is quite an impressive set of gear. But, of course, we have a very powerful enemy. Never go against him without first strapping on your equipment.

In football, not even Joe Montana ever tried anything that foolish. Don't try it in spiritual battle.

MOTTO

An ill-equipped Christian soldier is soon wounded.

1. What battles have I tried to fight in the past couple of weeks without my spiritual armor in place? How did I do?

2. Which pieces of armor do I need the most right now as I try to be the husband and father I need to be?

3. In addition to putting on armor, what does Ephesians 6:18 say I need to do to make it all work?

CALL TO ACTION

1. To whom will I be accountable in regard to my armor? Who will call me throughout the week and ask, "Do you have each piece of your armor on?"

2. In what three specific situations this next week do I need to have my armor on? Which pieces will be the most important in those situations?

Dear Lord, I praise you for designing this Satan-thwarting armor. Please help me to don this armor each day before I face the world. Help me to understand each piece and how it can guide me in my relationship with my wife and my kids. Also, help me to guide them to be armor-bearers as well.

THE THINK TANK

"Finally, brothers, whatever is true, whatever is noble, whatever is right, whatever is pure, whatever is lovely, whatever is admirable — if anything is excellent or praiseworthy — think about such things" (Philippians 4:8).

MARCHING ORDERS

FROM POINT MAN
Read: Chapter Four,
pages 100-102

FROM THE BIBLE
Read: Proverbs
21:20-29

Don't miss the significance of today's Bible verses:

•In Proverbs 21, we see the contrast between the fool and the wise. The wise thinks about things that bring good rewards; the foolish thinks about things that bring destruction.

•The wicked person tries to put up a front; the upright man carefully considers, or thinks about, his ways.

•In Philippians 4:8, we have a grocery list of right ways to think.

THINKING IT THROUGH

Have you ever talked to anyone who works for a think tank? It sounds like a weird concept, but it is really quite simple. These men and women are experts in a certain area, and their job is to do research on a topic, read all they can about it, talk it over with colleagues and other experts, and come to a conclusion on the area of concern. Essentially, they are paid to think.

It sounds like an odd idea because we either consider thinking to be such a natural part of our day that we can't believe someone is getting paid to do it, or we don't care a whole lot for the process so we can't imagine someone spending all day doing it.

No matter what we think of thinking — whether it gives us a headache or is something we love to sit around and do — we need to understand how important our thought life is to our marriage.

Proverbs 21:29 says, "an upright man gives thought to his ways." In other words, a wise person thinks through what he is going to do. He weighs the consequences or rewards of his actions. He thinks before he talks. He understands the ramifications of his actions. He knows how to think.

In addition to knowing how to think, we also must know what to think about. This is usually when we get into trouble.

Look at the pattern, as developed in James 1.

•Temptation: "each one is tempted when, by his own evil desire, he is dragged away and enticed" (verse 14).

•Desire: "after desire has conceived, it gives birth to sin" (verse 15).

•Sin: "sin, when it is full-grown, gives birth to death" (v. 15).

Sin starts in the mind. It starts with a thought — a desire, a concept — that comes from wrong thinking.

In other words, temptation can stare us in the face without harming us. But when we let that temptation become a thought or desire in our mind, we are pleading for big-time trouble. When our thought life harbors temptation and turns it into desire, sin is knocking at our door. And destruction is standing out there on the porch with it.

Because the danger of wrong thinking is so threatening to our well-being, we need a plan of attack to avoid it. Proverbs 21 gives us a good place to start by telling us to give thought to our ways. And Philippians 4:8 helps us finish the job by giving us a checklist of what we should think about.

Before we look at that checklist, though, we need to keep one other important truth in mind. We are not powerful enough in our own strength to clean out our own think tank and fill it with the good thoughts of Philippians 4. If we try to be self-cleaning in this regard, we'll fail. We must depend on the Holy Spirit to guide our thinking.

Romans 8:5 shows how this works: "Those who live according to the sinful nature have their minds set on what that nature desires; but those who live in accordance with the Spirit have their minds set on what the Spirit desires." So our first line of defense in the battle to protect our thought life is a strong dependence on the Holy Spirit to guide us.

The second line of defense depends on us. That's where Philippians 4:8 comes in. Let's look at the positive things we should think about if we want to eliminate the negative thinking that can lead to sin and destruction:

• *Think about true things.* This begins with God's Word, which is completely true and comes from the One who is Truth. Therefore, what we think about needs to be filtered through the grid of scriptural truth. Any thinking that contradicts the guidelines of God's Word is trouble.

• *Think about what is noble.* According to the *American Heritage Dictionary,* "noble" means "having or showing qualities of high moral character, such as courage, generosity, or honor." Much of the problem with the thought life of today's Christian is all the time spent pursuing ignoble entertainment. Far too much of what is in the mind of believers would hardly be considered "showing qualities of high moral character." Avoiding the bad and filling our minds with the good is what this part of Philippians 4:8 is all about.

• *Think about what is right.* Honesty starts in the mind. If our desire is to speak the truth in love, we must keep honest, aboveboard thoughts on our minds.

• *Think about what is pure.* The love of God is pure. A monogamous marital relationship is pure. Heaven is pure. A father's love for his children is pure. There is so much to think about that is pure, we shouldn't take time for any alternatives.

• *Think about what is lovely.* No, this is not an invitation to pine over Miss America. The lovely things of this world are those created by God for His glory. For instance, we are told that the feet of those who spread the gospel are beautiful (Romans 10:15). The creation and God's created are wonders to behold, and our appreciation of them reflects our love for him.

• *Think about what is admirable.* Sadly, there is so much in our world today that needs a brown wrapper around it. Stuff that was once relegated to back corner alleys and smelly dives is now presented as acceptable for our consumption. We need to ferret out the things not worth admiring and keep them out of our minds.

• *Think about what is excellent and praiseworthy.* All good things come from God, and all goodness is a result of His handiwork. Therefore, whatever is godly and good reflects God and deserves our attention and praise. To keep focused on godliness, we need to avoid what is ungodly and not worthy of praise.

Just as wrong thoughts are the grenades of the enemy, so right thoughts are weapons from God to use against the attacks of our foe, Satan.

If we fill our think tank with ideas, concepts, mental pictures, imaginations, and information that fit into Philippians 4:8, we avoid danger and build for ourselves a thought life that pleases and honors God. And isn't that the main purpose of our existence?

MOTTO

A pure think tank leaves plenty of room for God.

1. Are my thoughts God's thoughts, or do I keep them as my own private domain?

2. Who am I fooling if I believe I can have wrong thoughts and keep anyone from finding out about them?

3. In what way does my exposure to the media affect my thought life?

CALL TO ACTION

1. If I took all of the traits of Philippians 4:8 and turned them into opposites, which would more accurately characterize my thinking?

true	false
noble	ignoble
right	wrong
pure	filthy
lovely	ugly
admirable	shameful
praiseworthy	disgraceful

2. The next time I watch a TV program, I will keep track of what is said and shown, using Philippians 4:8 (and its opposites) as my checklists.

3. What was the best thought I had today? The worst?

Lord, please protect my thinking. Hedge me around with the Spirit to help me avoid wrong thoughts. Keep me focused on Jesus. Direct me away from anything that will plant wrong thoughts in my head.

EAT YOUR BIBLE!

"How sweet are your promises to my taste, sweeter than honey to my mouth!" (Psalm 119:103).

MARCHING ORDERS

FROM POINT MAN
Read: Chapter Five,
pages 109-18

FROM THE BIBLE
Read: Psalm
119:97–104

As you read today's Scripture passage, consider this:

•By speaking of the Bible as something tasty, the psalmist reiterates how appealing it should be to us.

•Look at what the Bible can do: give insight, provide understanding, suggest right living.

•Notice the attitudes toward the Bible exhibited in these verses: affection, dedication, appreciation, obedience.

THINKING IT THROUGH

If you are what you eat, then I suppose I should be a quarter-pounder with cheese with a side order of fries. I've surely had enough of those drive-through specialties to give me sesame seed buns.

Seriously, every time the *New England Journal of Medicine* comes out with another study on the eating habits of Americans, it becomes clearer that if we don't wise up in our eating habits, we're *all* going to have clogged arteries. We may not begin to look like fettuccine with alfredo sauce after prolonged exposure to fat-laden foods, but our insides know the difference.

Our physical health mirrors our eating habits.

And because our eating habits generally gravitate toward food that has more of the things we shouldn't eat, we tend to be overweight and fat-urated.

Good food often leads to bad results.

Not so in our spiritual life.

The best food we can possibly consume for our inner person — the Word of God — is the most delicious food available.

Yet we are often guilty of stuffing ourselves on the junk food of the world — reading and watching productions that do nothing but make us fat, lazy, complacent Christians. And all the time we are munching on the world's goodies, the best food sits neglected on our bookshelf.

Recently, a study of American soldiers revealed that troops who are sent into action often find themselves at less than top efficiency simply because they don't eat enough. Although they can have all the meals-ready-to-eat that they want, they seem to need more substance. Therefore, the Army is contemplating setting up more sophisticated field mess halls where the soldiers can get better meals than they can get out of those drab packets.

Spiritually, we need to realize that our feeding from God's Word cannot consist of snacks, 30-second readings from a booklet, and quick pre-meal prayers. If we are interested in becoming battle-ready, we need to pull up at the mess hall of God's Word and dive in for a real meal.

That's apparently what the psalmist did. Look at what he said! "I meditate on it all day long" (Psalm 119:97). That's not a quick meal. That's a feast!

It can be done. Let's say you find a verse from today's reading that intrigues and challenges you. Write it down on a 3"x 5" card or on a Post-It® note. Then take it with you. When you hop in the truck to go to work, put it on the dash. Think about it when you stop at traffic lights.

Ask yourself some questions about it:

1. To whom was God directing this verse?
2. What does this verse mean?
3. What applications does it have for me?
4. What am I going to do today?

Then, at the end of the day, either on the way home or at night before retiring, review the verse. Ask yourself:

1. What does this verse mean? (Review.)
2. How did I apply this verse today?

Tomorrow, find another verse to take with you.

Without too much effort, you will find that you can say, "I meditate on God's Word all day long." Think of what that will do for your spiritual health!

The more you eat God's Word, the more like Jesus Christ you will become in your thinking. The characteristics listed in today's passage are clearly Christlike, obvious signs of spiritual health.

Feasting on God's teachings gives us:

• *More wisdom than our enemies.* Remember that when Solomon had the opportunity to ask for anything, he asked for wisdom. In today's world, that ability to use knowledge is still immensely valuable.

• *More insight than our teachers.* Recall when Jesus was twelve years old and confounded the teachers in the synagogue? That was not a show-off time for him. It simply meant that his knowledge of Scripture far exceeded theirs, and rightly so. We need a vast knowledge of Scripture too — not to confound people, but to have at our disposal so we can instill right values in our children.

• *More understanding than our elders.* In this verse, the crux is obedience. Obeying God's precepts and principles in today's society means going against the grain. Yet a man of understanding does so.

•*Protection from the evil path.* Are you familiar with 2 Timothy 3:16? It says that the Word of God is given to us for a variety of reasons, including "correcting and training in righteousness." A thorough knowledge of the Bible helps us avoid the pitfalls of sin.

•*A sweet taste in our mouths.* Look at all the books on your shelf. Is there any book that gives you such a comforting, surrounding feeling as the very Word of God? Relish it.

How's your spiritual health? Feeling a bit anemic? Run down? Worn out? Not feeling like you can fight the spiritual battles you face each day?

Then belly up to the table. Dig in to God's Word. Take all you want — big helpings, seconds, the works.

You'll love the taste and soon find you have more spiritual energy than you ever thought possible.

MOTTO

Nothing tastes sweeter and is more energizing than
a generous helping of God's Word.

DEBRIEFING

1. What is my average daily intake of God's Word? Is that not enough or just right?

2. If I asked my pastor for a spiritual checkup, how healthy would I be? How close would the correlation be between my spiritual health and my biblical intake?

3. Whom do I know who is a real student of the Word? What benefits is he enjoying that I want to starting enjoying too?

CALL TO ACTION

1. For the next week, I'll try Steve's 3"x 5" card suggestion. The passage I will meditate on is _____.

2. If I've never read the Bible through, I will do so by

_____.

3. To increase my understanding of Scripture, I will obtain which of the following supplemental materials?

___ The Bible on tape
___ Sermons on tape
___ A Bible study guide
___ A study Bible
___ A notebook

Dear Lord, thank you for your Word. Thank you for preserving it for thousands of years so I can read it today. Please help me schedule time with the Bible each day. Teach me to love it and to gain understanding from it. Help me to grow stronger through the teaching of your Word.

WHAT A BOOK!

"The word of the Lord stands forever" (1 Peter 1:25).

MARCHING ORDERS

FROM POINT MAN
Read: Chapter Five,
pages 112-114

FROM THE BIBLE
Read: 2 Peter 1:16-21

As you read today's Bible verses, ask yourself:

• What is the significance of Peter's mentioning that he and others were eyewitness observers of Jesus' life?

• The message of the gospel does not consist of "cleverly invented stories." How do other religious accounts differ from Christianity in this area?

• The prophecies of Scripture were not man-made, but were instead given directly by the Holy Spirit. Why is that important?

THINKING IT THROUGH

Not long ago, a researcher investigating the papers and belongings of Martin Luther discovered a rare find. As he went through a library containing Luther's books, he found a Bible Luther used for his own personal study, complete with his handwritten notations.

Imagine the joy of that researcher when he first understood what he had found. I can imagine him sitting back in his chair to contemplate the significance of this book. His hands must have shaken and his mind must have raced with the many ways this book would change his life. He must have hurried to find a way to protect his discovery, and he must have quickly contacted friends to tell them. Because this Bible contained the Great Reformer's words, observations, and thoughts, it was of inestimable value.

The irony of that situation can be found in one simple fact: That Bible was of priceless value before Martin Luther ever picked it up back in the early part of the 16th century.

The Bible, no matter who owns it, is the most valuable document ever penned or printed.

Everything of value I have said in this book or in *Point Man* is based on the Bible. Without the Bible, we have no standards, no basis for leading our families, no hope for the future, no salvation, and no direction in this life.

That's why we need to stop occasionally and reaffirm in our thinking just how remarkable the Bible is. We need to recapture the awe that should exist in our hearts as we think of what we are holding when we take the Bible in our hands.

The Bible is remarkable in its inspiration. As Peter mentions in 2 Peter 1:21, God originated the words of Scripture and the Holy Spirit guided them to be written. In 2 Timothy 3:16, Paul reminds us that Scripture is "God-breathed," which means that the writers were guided by God's Holy Spirit to pen the words they put on a scroll.

The Bible is remarkable in its creation. It took well over a millennium for the text of the Bible to be penned by its more than forty human writers. But it takes just one word to describe its theme: redemption. It is a sure sign of God's hand of guidance that more than three dozen men could write sixty-six related documents in a span of 1,500 years and create a book that is so tightly woven together in every way.

The Bible is remarkable in its honesty. If you were David, wouldn't you want the author of the Samuel scrolls to leave out that little story about Bathsheba? Or if you were Peter, wouldn't you prefer that the gospel writers conveniently forgot about your denial of Jesus? But the Bible tells all. It even reveals that Jesus was angry at the moneychangers in the temple and cried over Jerusalem. In God's wisdom, he inspired the writers to present stories and persons just as they were.

The Bible is remarkable in its power. No other book has ever come close to being as widely distributed as the Bible. No other book has guided so many civilizations in their creation of laws and standards as has the Bible. No other book has been so censured by governments yet always made a comeback. Whenever the Bible has gone into a new civilization, lives have been changed. Other books inform or entertain or inspire, but only God's Book transforms lives, communities, and countries.

When we hold the Bible in our hands, do we ever approach the wonder and awe of that researcher who discovered Martin Luther's Bible? Only if we have a high view of God's written Word will we develop the right attitude toward the value of its teaching. Only then will we work hard to incorporate its teachings into our lives. And only then will we spend the time with the Bible necessary to begin to understand the mind of God.

Think of all the ways we get information today. We have books, magazines, newspapers, e-mail, the Internet, letters, radio, television, movies, videos, and CD-Rom. We have interoffice memos, newsletters, advertising tabloids, and billboards. It is easy to get distracted by all of that and forget that sitting on our shelf is the living Word of the living God — a personal message from him to us.

The Almighty God of the universe has spoken through the Bible. The answers to life's most important questions are printed on its pages. The history of the world is recorded in it. The future destiny of all people is spelled out on its pages. Its chapters contain guidelines for living successfully.

Hold your Bible with a new sense of awe. What a Book it is!

If you can't get excited about God's Word, you can't get excited!

1. What does the fact of inspiration do for me when I read the Bible?

2. What is the most remarkable aspect of the Bible to me?

3. What is my favorite passage of Scripture? How does that passage challenge me?

CALL TO ACTION

1. To help me in my appreciation of God's Word, I will do one of the following:

    a. Commit to read through the Bible in a year.

    b. Obtain a Bible handbook, study guide, or other help to assist my study.

    c. Start a regular reading time each day in which I take notes.

    d. Join a small group Bible study.

2. I will read a book that can tell me more about the inspiration of the Bible and how we got it.

3. Here are five specific things God's Word has done for me or taught me:

    a. _____

    b. _____

    c. _____

    d. _____

    e. _____

Thank you, Lord, for giving us your Word. Thanks for not making us drift along without help and without hope. Please guide me to a new appreciation for your Word and help me to understand it better. Please don't allow me to take for granted what you have provided in and through the Bible.

A HANDBOOK, NOT AN ENCYCLOPEDIA

"Do not merely listen to the word, and so deceive yourselves. Do what it says" (James 1:22).

MARCHING ORDERS

FROM POINT MAN
Read: Chapter Five,
pages 118-21

FROM THE BIBLE
Read: James 1:21–27

In today's brief Bible reading, don't miss these points:

•Something is deceptive about listening to the Word but not obeying it.

•Just as we don't use a mirror once and then disregard it, nor should we only glance at God's Word and quickly forget what it says.

•A close connection exists between getting rid of bad things and accepting the good of the Word of God.

THINKING IT THROUGH

From the *Grolier's Encyclopedia* comes this definition:

The word Bible *is derived from the Greek* biblia, *meaning "books," and refers to the sacred writings of Judaism and Christianity. The Bible consists of two parts. The first part, called the Old Testament by Christians, consists of the sacred writings of the Jewish people.... The second part, called the New Testament, records the story of Jesus and the beginnings of Christianity.*

Fairly interesting, but not very inspiring.

That's because treating the Bible as simply a book among other books diminishes its value. And when we diminish its value, we are less likely to search its pages for the life-giving, spirit-strengthening messages it contains. Our spiritual growth depends in large part on getting into the Word regularly and seriously.

Consider the last book you read, other than the Bible. Perhaps it was a mystery that intrigued, entertained, even surprised you. Or maybe it was a historical account of the Civil War or another important event. It could have even been a popular how-to book, written from a Christian perspective.

As valuable as those books are, they cannot begin to provide the sustenance that God's Word gives.

Imagine life without a word from God:

•No word about the salvation he has provided.

•No explanation of our origins.

•No hint of God's working throughout human history.

•No clear guidelines for living found in such passages as the Ten Commandments and the Sermon on the Mount.

•No concept of what the future holds.

•No principles for marriage and family.

•No foundation for our worship of God.

•No knowledge of prayer's power.

Think of the advantages you enjoy solely because God left us His Word. Then contemplate life without those advantages.

But what's more startling is how often we fail to take advantage of what God has provided.

Where you work, your employer has probably provided you with an employee manual. Enclosed within its pages are all the things you need to know about vacation days, sick days, how to dress for work, who's in charge, where to park your car, how to file a complaint, what your insurance covers, and a multitude of other things.

Now, you probably don't take that thing home with you at night and pore over it while other family members are out playing basketball in the driveway. But you do need to know what is inside. If it says you can't wear jeans to work and you show up one day in your favorite Levi's, you can't claim ignorance. You are expected to know what is in the handbook.

Likewise, we are expected to know what is in God's Word. And beyond that, we are expected to obey it.

The Bible as literature is a great course to take in school, but it's not a very effective course to take in life. God's Word was designed for much more than its literary beauty, of which there is a considerable amount. The Bible is meant to be implemented, as 2 Timothy 3:16 teaches. This verse is similar to an employer putting a notice in the employee manual that says:

THESE ARE THE RULES FOR THIS SHOP. THEY WERE CREATED BY THE MANAGEMENT FOR THE GOOD OF ALL EMPLOYEES.

God's version of that disclaimer goes more like this:

EVERYTHING IN THIS BOOK COMES FROM GOD. THE CONTENTS WILL TEACH YOU, REBUKE YOU, CORRECT YOU, AND TRAIN YOU TO LIVE RIGHTEOUSLY, ENABLING YOU TO DO EVERY GOOD WORK.

The happy consequences of doing what an employer asks you to do include such benefits as a good working relationship, continued pay increases, and a positive outlook on the job.

In God's economy, there's an even greater advantage to living by the handbook. In James 1, the writer reveals that the person who looks into God's handbook and obeys what he reads will receive God's blessing on his activities (verse 25).

You can't get that from an encyclopedia — or from any other book on your shelf, for that matter.

Take up the challenge to study God's Word itself. Find out what God is saying to you each day and then put His words into practice. It's the best (and only) way to enjoy His blessings on your life.

DEBRIEFING

1. How faithful have I been recently in reading the Bible? Has the amount of time I have spent with it provided me the opportunity to look "intently into the perfect law" (James 1:25)?

2. What are some specific life questions I have been wondering about — questions that I need to search the Scriptures for if I want the answers?

3. If I were to measure my spiritual strength on the basis of my devotion to God's Word, would I be a 102-pound weakling, Arnold Schwarzanegger, or somewhere in between?

CALL TO ACTION

1. This week I will get a notebook and begin to journal my Bible reading time, noting the specific life-application principles I find. After a week of doing this, I will check to see if I am using the "mirror" or just looking into it and forgetting what I have seen.

2. Do I need an accountability partner to check up on this project? How will I encourage a fellow Christian to do the same?

Dear heavenly Father, author of the Scriptures, thank you for leaving us with your handbook for successful living. Thank you for its accuracy and trustworthiness. Please help me to search its pages for the truths you want me to live by.

FAIL TO PLAN; PLAN TO FAIL

"I rise before dawn and cry for help; I have put my hope in your word" (Psalm 119:147).

MARCHING ORDERS

FROM POINT MAN
Read: Chapter Five,
pages 121-131

FROM THE BIBLE
Read: Psalm
119:145-152

Don't miss the significance of today's Scripture reading:

•The psalmist mentioned specifics in his devotion to God, including complete openness (verse 145), obedience (verse 145), and a definite time to meet with God (verse 147).

•The psalmist was under attack from an outside force, yet instead of going after that force, he was depending on God for help.

•Notice, at the end, what the psalmist understood to be true about God's laws.

THINKING IT THROUGH

Isn't it great to watch a sports team that has a specific game plan? The coaches have worked hard all week to devise a scheme that will counter and negate the opponent's strengths and emphasize their own. Often, a good game plan will enable a team of less potential, talent, and reputation to gain the advantage.

Some time ago, a high school basketball team with lots of

advantages was scheduled to play for the district championship against a team it had twice defeated during the season by more than twenty-five points. The first team had height, poise, scoring balance, and a winning streak. The other team had won five games all season.

Yet the coach of the poorer team had a flawless game plan. He had his players stall — holding the ball for minutes at a time. Even early in the game, when the plan didn't appear to be working, the coach adamantly refused to give in.

No matter what the score, his team simply walked it up the court and held onto it.

This frustrated the better team, and they began to rush things at their end. Over and over they made mistakes, simply out of frustration. Slowly the poorer team came back with its slow offense and an occasional burst of scoring.

In the end, the unranked, unsung, unheralded team won the game by a single point in overtime. The game plan worked.

In a sense, we are like that team with the bad record. We are underdogs in our world. Like the writer of Psalm 119, we live in a society full of wicked schemes, intent on destroying our spiritual life, our marriage, our home.

If we were to concentrate on the power of the opposing forces, we would be afraid to go out for warmups.

But to devise a game plan that will help us defeat the enemy, let's look at David's plan for getting the most out of his relationship with God.

Strategy 1: Make meditation of God's Word a constant in your life. Psalm 1:2 describes a man whose "delight is in the law of the Lord, and on his law he meditates day and night." In Psalm 119:97 the same idea is repeated. This is not a call to monkish separation from real life, but a declaration that throughout the day we need to have God's Word on our mind. As we do, we can think about — meditate on — how it should affect our words and deeds. Just as Paul says we should pray without ceasing

(1 Thessalonians 5:17), suggesting a continual awareness of our communication with God, so David is saying we need to be in continual awareness of what God's Word is saying to us.

Strategy 2: Have a set-apart time to meet with God. In Psalm 119:147, David says, "I rise before dawn and cry for help." Of course, reading those words may not be a real encouragement, especially if you are one of those men who equate the sunrise with punishment. If you're not a morning person, though, don't be thrown off.

It doesn't matter what time of day we meet with God, it matters that we do.

Some have suggested that time with God is important enough to merit an entry in your daily calendar. Not a bad idea, for it says, "I have an appointment and I'd better be there."

Other people set aside additional times to communicate with God or learn more about Him. One pastor of a large church, when offered a car phone from a friend, turned it down because he used his time in the car for prayer, listening to Christian music, and catching up on sermons of others on tape. His car time was set aside as a time alone with God.

Strategy 3: Plan the time well to avoid the usual pitfalls. Time alone with God can be immensely valuable. For taking a nap, for instance. Or brainstorming about your problems at work. Or daydreaming about your next vacation. Or. . . well, you get the idea.

It's just you, your Bible, your notebook, and God. Poor planning sometimes reduces it to just you.

To get the most of your devotional times:

•Bring along a specific prayer list, and pray in bursts, not in long sessions.

•Have a pre-designed plan for Bible reading, whether a through-the-Bible plan, a devotional guide, or a workbook.

•As you read the Bible, take notes of what it says, what it means, what questions it raises, and how you can apply it to your life.

•Change positions as you pray. Stand up. Kneel down. Pray out loud. Do whatever it takes to keep your concentration strong as you pray.

•Incorporate singing into your time with God. If singing in the showers is okay, how about singing about the showers of blessing God has rained on you? (Your family will forgive you.)

David knew God intimately. According to Psalm 119, his relationship with the Lord seemed to be one of openness and straightforwardness. He trusted God's words and God's laws. He felt God's closeness.

As we go up against the battles that threaten us each day, our best chance for success is based on our having that kind of human-divine relationship. And that relationship comes when we keep the lines of communication open with God.

Put together a plan and work it. And then watch God make you a winner.

MOTTO

If our most important appointment is with God,
He will take care of the rest.

DEBRIEFING

1. As I think about developing a plan for my personal devotions with God, what seem to be the biggest obstacles? What would God have me do to tear down those barriers?

2. What excites me the most about the possibilities of a planned time with God? From past experience, what has been my biggest blessing?

CALL TO ACTION

1. For the next week, I will write my appointment with God in my daily planner. Then I will develop an outline of how I can best spend that time.

2. Passages of study:

    a. _____

    b. _____

    c. _____

    d. _____

    e. _____

3. Prayer requests:

    a. _____

    b. _____

    c. _____

    d. _____

    e. _____

Dear Father, please help me as I try to spend more time with you. Thank you that you are always available. Help me to set aside more time to spend in your Word.

PLACES FOR THE HEART

"Blessed is the man who does not walk in the counsel of the wicked or stand in the way of sinners or sit in the seat of mockers. But his delight is in the law of the Lord, and on his law he meditates day and night" (Psalm 1:1–2).

MARCHING ORDERS

FROM POINT MAN
Read: Chapter Five,
pages 127-128

FROM THE BIBLE
Read: Psalm 63

As you read today's Bible verses, consider this:

• According to Psalm 63, our pursuit of God is like a thirst — something that drives us to Him like a thirsty man in a desert seeks water.

• It helps us to go to God's sanctuary, whatever that might mean in our situation.

• The satisfaction of the soul comes with the offering of praise.

• Meditation recognizes God as the source of help and protection.

THINKING IT THROUGH

A visiting preacher asked a church congregation for a show of hands to indicate who among the crowd prayed regularly. Hands shot up all over as people eagerly said yes to that question.

Then he asked the worshipers how many of them meditated

regularly. Among the hundreds of pewsters, only a few scattered respondents waved back at the speaker.

"That's the response I always get," the preacher said. "We know how to pray, but we don't know how to meditate."

Indeed, we might even be afraid of meditation. We've all heard how bad some forms of meditation are. Yoga and transcendental meditation are examples of meditation that would tend to mess us up more than help us. We associate most kinds of deep thinking exercises with some cultic or Eastern religion, so we avoid them like a pair of plaid pants.

Yet there are several clear biblical calls for us to do some meditating. Passages like Psalm 1 and Psalm 63, as well as Psalm 19:14, Psalm 77:12, and Joshua 1:8, suggest that getting involved mentally in Scripture is important.

If meditation isn't something we've learned in Sunday school like we have prayer, Bible reading, witnessing, and other spiritual disciplines, perhaps a quick lesson in the subject would be beneficial.

To *meditate* means to "reflect on or to engage in contemplation, especially of a spiritual or devotional nature; to consider carefully and at length." Synonyms of *meditate* are words such as *reflect, think through,* and *ponder.*

Like the preacher asked, we need to ask ourselves, "When was the last time we took time to consider a Bible passage at length, to spend time reflecting and pondering what God's Word tells us?"

Throughout the course of *Point Man* and this devotional book, I've asked you to do a lot of things. And I realize that throwing another new concept your way might have you wishing you could reach through the pages, tap me on the shoulder and say, "Hey, man! Enough already! I can't keep up with all this stuff!"

Yet I feel strongly that this concept is so important that I'll risk overload to tell you about it. Remember that all we know of God and His plans for us comes from his Word. Therefore, if we truly want His marching orders, we need to dig for them. We need to read His words and think about their affect on us; we need to listen to Him talk to us through those words. And that takes time. That takes meditation.

Think about the benefits of biblical meditation. According to Psalm 1, a meditator is firmly rooted and fruitful. Psalm 63 suggests that a meditator remains in the safety of God's "wings" and is upheld by God's "right hand." Joshua 1:8 promises prosperity and success for the one who dwells on the Word. Those benefits we would all do well to seek.

But how do we meditate on a passage? Do we read it, sit with our legs folded, and wait to be zapped with some incredible inside scoop?

Let me suggest a few meditation pointers that may increase the value of your dedicated Bible study time.

1. Find a quiet place, free of distractions.

2. Take along a notebook.

3. Have access to a study Bible with notes.

4. Pray before reading, asking for the Holy Spirit to give you understanding.

5. Read the passage completely through one time.

6. Make a list of questions that the passage raised in your mind. Go through the passage and try to answer those questions.

7. Find a single theme for the passage. This is not always possible when reading a narrative, but it can usually be done.

8. Find a verse that suggests the theme and spend a few minutes memorizing it.

9. Ask yourself a series of questions:
   a. To whom was this passage originally written?
   b. What was the author telling those people?
   c. How does this passage relate to me and my understanding of God's working in my life?
   d. Is this passage meant to lead me to praise God, obey God, understand God, or seek God?

e. If God had written this passage for no one else but me, what would He want me to know or do?

10. Pray again, this time asking God to help you apply this passage to your life in the way He intended it.

11. Throughout the rest of the day, think back about the passage, trying to recall its implications, its theme, and its key verse.

The Word of God is indeed full of places for the heart. We can read what the Bible says, using our head to understand the words and even comprehend the concepts, but until we make the Word a part of our heart — of our inner being — we will probably go away from our Bible study unaffected. To meditate on God's Word allows us the time and the heart-to-heart effort to get to know our heavenly Father better and to understand His will for us.

As leaders in our families, our work sites, and our communities — as busy men with more responsibilities than we have time for — one of the best uses of our time is to meditate on God's Word. We can spend no better preparation time than to spend time in God's places for the heart.

MOTTO

To know God, know God's Word.

DEBRIEFING

1. How does the concept of meditation sound to me? Is this an extra burden that I don't have time for, or does it have a certain appeal?

2. What other things in life do I meditate on? What value do I find in that kind of concentrated thinking?

3. When was the last time I earnestly sought God and thirsted after a more thorough knowledge of Him?

CALL TO ACTION

1. Is there an intriguing Scripture passage that I have loved and longed to understand more fully? When will I set aside time to meditate on that passage?

2. What are some additional questions I will ask about a passage I'm meditating on?

"O God, you are my God, earnestly I seek you; my soul thirsts for you, my body longs for you, in a dry and weary land where there is no water. I have seen you in the sanctuary and beheld your power and your glory. Because your love is better than life, my lips will glorify you" (Psalm 63:1–3).

PRESEASON TRAINING

"Peter stood up with the Eleven, raised his voice and addressed the crowd..." (Acts 2:14).

FROM POINT MAN
Read: Chapter Six, pages 133-146

FROM THE BIBLE
Read: Acts 2:14–41

• Think about what you know about Peter before this incident. Compare what he is doing on this day with some of the less-than-stellar events in his life before this.

• As you think back on Peter's days before Jesus was crucified, reflect on how much he had to change to be the bold Christian leader he became.

THINKING IT THROUGH

Peter and the other disciples should have worn little badges that said, "Apostle In Training." Throughout the time they were sitting at Jesus' feet, listening to him, helping him with the crowds, and sharing hour upon hour with him, Jesus was preparing them for a day they could know nothing about.

They often seem befuddled by some of the things he was trying to tell them. The problem was that Jesus could see beyond the cross to what he had planned for them, while they could only see what was happening right then.

It was a time of preseason training for them. Jesus was getting them ready for the time when he would be gone from this earth and they would have to propagate Christianity all by themselves.

Think about it. After Jesus was taken from the sight of the apostles as recorded in Acts 1, the future of our faith hung in the balance. If these eleven men, as well as some women, Jesus' mother Mary, and his brothers (Acts 1:13–14), had not convinced others of the importance of faith in Jesus, Christianity would have died.

But Jesus had trained them well — especially Peter. Despite his failures during the preseason, when he needed to throw out the opening pitch, Peter had his delivery down perfectly.

In the very first evangelistic meeting ever held, three thousand people came to a saving knowledge of Jesus Christ.

We all understand the importance of preseason training. Oh, we may not put much stock in the scores of spring training baseball games because they don't count, but we know that what goes on to get ready for those games is vital. Imagine the disadvantage a team would have if the players were to show up on the first day of the season without any training. On the other hand, a team could go 0-20 in the spring yet begin winning on opening day and stay in first place all year because of superior talent and great conditioning.

Preseason training, then, is vital!

Now, we may not have the future of the Christian faith in our hands as Peter did that day as he addressed the folks at Solomon's Colonnade in Jerusalem, but we have too much at stake in our lives to skip the training.

We must be in shape spiritually to guide our family in godliness. We must be in shape spiritually if we want to be an effective witness for Jesus — thus duplicating the ministry of Peter. We must be in shape spiritually, or we could fall before the enemy's onslaught.

Have you ever been to a fantasy baseball camp?

What the camp directors try to do is simulate for the campers what it is major leaguers go through at spring training. It can be a painful time for guys who grew up on Stan Musial and Willie Mays. Their "preseason" regimen might consist of the following:

1. *Exercises and running.* The goal is to get campers in shape for the games to follow.

2. *Instruction and training.* Guys who really know what they're doing try to help guys who really don't know what they're doing.

3. *Practice.* The rust flies off the old moves as the pros hit grounders and fly balls to the fielders and throw batting practice to the hitters.

4. *Game experience.* The testing ground for the campers comes when they have to stand in against the big leaguers at the plate or try to field their hitting.

When we move off the field and into real life, we need the same elements of preseason training if we want to win spiritually. If we want to have an impact on a world that doesn't know much about our faith — just like the society of Peter's day — we have to get moving.

The apostle Paul made that clear when he said, "Everyone who competes...goes into strict training" (1 Corinthians 9:25). Our strict training should include these preseason activities:

1. *Exercises and running.* "Run in such a way as to get the prize," Paul tells us (1 Corinthians 9:24). We can't do that if we don't exercise our mind through reading God's Word faithfully.

2. *Instruction and training.* Through the words of Scripture and the advice of wise Christian friends and counselors, we learn how we are to compete in this race. Those pointers help us make wise decisions and avoid potential problem areas.

3. *Practice.* Within the safe confines of our homes, we have many opportunities to talk about our Lord, to work on memorizing Scripture, to discuss spiritual issues — all as preparation to taking the Word to the world.

4. *Game situations.* Once Jesus left, it was up to Peter to

become the spokesman for the faith. Likewise, we become Jesus' representatives in the world. Are we ready for the big time, or do we need some more practice?

Peter had no idea what impact his speech would have that first Pentecost Sunday. But he was ready because he had been trained by Jesus, and his message was a tremendous success.

How ready are you to make a stand for Jesus?

MOTTO

Jesus was ready to lay down his life for us, we should be ready to stand up for him.

DEBRIEFING

1. If I had to declare my readiness for the tasks God has for me as I serve Him, would I say I'm ready, still in training, or way out of shape?

2. In which spiritual discipline do I feel weakest: prayer, Bible reading and meditation, witnessing, or church attendance?

CALL TO ACTION

1. In the next month, I will take an opportunity to speak out for the Savior, whether by teaching a Sunday school lesson, witnessing to a neighbor, or writing a letter to the editor. But I will first spend some time in training, making myself ready.

2. I will honestly ask myself, "Have I taken on the leadership role in my home that God has been preparing me for?" Then I will work harder to accept my role, which will force me to keep in tune with God.

Dear God, thank you that Peter was willing to be trained under Jesus—and then stand up for the faith at Pentecost. Please help me to look to Jesus for the spiritual training I need so I can be a witness for Jesus and an example to my family.

A PRAYER PRIMER

"This, then, is how you should pray: 'Our Father in heaven, hallowed be your name. . . '" (Matthew 6:9).

MARCHING ORDERS

FROM POINT MAN
Read: Chapter Six,
pages 140-142

FROM THE BIBLE
Read: Matthew 6:5–15

In today's brief Bible reading, don't miss these points:

• Jesus gave some preliminary instructions about prayer before he gave his listeners an example of proper prayer.

• The Lord spoke an intriguing truth when he said, "your Father knows what you need before you ask Him" (verse 8).

• The prayer example Jesus gave his listeners contains the elements of praise, petition, provision, and penitence.

THINKING IT THROUGH

There are prayers, and there are PRAYERS. You've heard the all-capital PRAYERS, I'm sure. The ones that you sometimes hear in church on a Sunday morning. The ones that start at the church, go completely around the world to every mission outpost imaginable, and end up back home through some mysterious, circuitous route. The ones that try the will power of young children who know they are supposed to remain still with their head bowed but whose bodies are screaming out for action.

I'm glad Jesus didn't pray one of those prayers when his listeners asked him how to pray. No, when Jesus was given the opportunity to show his followers how to pray, he practiced that greatest of all rhetorical devices: brevity.

In just a few words, he demonstrated for them — and us — the essence of talking with the Father.

This is not to say that long prayers are bad (except in the opinion of fidgety children). In fact, Jesus himself prayed a rather lengthy prayer recorded in John 17.

But as a teaching tool, Jesus' prayer in Matthew 6 is instructive in its brevity and clarity.

Prayer. Talking with God. Communicating with the Creator of the universe. Expressing our heart to our heavenly Father. However we refer to it, prayer is our vital link to the One who loved us and redeemed us.

Because of his greatness, majesty, power, and glory, we want to make sure to address the Lord the way He wants to be addressed. And because of our love for Him, our devotion to Him, and our respect for Him, we want to address Him in a way that indicates our heartfelt admiration. Both of those elements are found in the prayer that Jesus modeled for us.

Because God is our Jehovah-Jireh, our provider, we need to know how to ask good gifts of Him. Because God is our Redeemer, we need to know how to approach Him when we need his mercy and grace. Again, both of those elements are found in the passage we call the Lord's Prayer.

Let's look closer at this primer to see what we can learn about the proper elements of a prayer that pleases God.

•*Acknowledgement of God's fatherhood.* Politically correct, inclusive language notwithstanding, God is our Father. We are His adopted children, brought into the family through the redemptive power of the death, burial, and resurrection of Jesus Christ. For those of us who know have come into a relationship with God through Jesus, He is our Father in the perfect sense of the word.

•*Honor and respect his name.* God is not the man upstairs or the big guy in the sky. In Exodus 20, we find out how special God's name is: "You shall not misuse the name of the LORD your God..." (verse 7). Prayer honors God when we speak lovingly and respectfully of Him, always being aware that simply speaking his name is a privilege.

To use His name in any other context than honor and respect must surely grieve God's heart. To use it as an expletive or oath sets us up as hypocrites when we go to pray. Therefore it is not just in times of prayer that we need to guard our tongues. God's name is always to be hallowed.

•*Acknowledgement of God's sovereignty.* When we ask for God's will to be done — either in our lives or when we ask for God's kingdom to come — we are taking our hands off our life and giving it to Him. Prayer should always be an opportunity to tell God again that our life is dedicated to His service and that we are open to doing whatever He wants us to do.

•*Trusting God for today's provisions.* It is ironic that in our day of affluence and plenty we have a hard time understanding this concept. In Jesus' day, the folks knew about their daily bread. Each day they were required to get provisions for that day. Not only could they ill afford to stock up on two weeks' worth of groceries, but they also had no way of keeping food fresh. Therefore each day meant a trip to the market to get that day's provisions. That's still true in many countries today.

In this country, however, we can have food enough in the house for a month and still not feel we are stocked well enough. Whether with provisions or life itself, all God ever promises us on this earth is today. Tomorrow is always an added bonus.

When we keep that in mind, we can be more thankful for "our daily bread."

•*Asking for forgiveness.* God's willingness to forgive is astounding. Whereas we humans like to hold on to grudges and find all kinds of reasons why we shouldn't forgive, God is always willing to forgive. Yet there is a stipulation mentioned here. In this passage and in others, Jesus reminds us that if we seek forgiveness, we first need to forgive others who have wronged us.

Race car driver Darrell Waltrip had gotten into a shouting match with fellow driver Ricky Craven. A couple of weeks later, Darrell was asked to pray in the drivers' Sunday chapel. He stood up and said, "I can't do this until I do something else first." He then called Craven to the front and asked for his forgiveness. Then he prayed.

In prayer we ask for God's forgiveness, but first, we must ask for the forgiveness of those we have offended.

•*Asking for protection.* In this dangerous world we live in, we can easily walk right into temptation. We can be led by "the evil one" to take paths of destruction, away from the One who protects us. Or, we can pray to God for guidance — we can ask for Him to direct our paths. We can't afford to be too proud to ask for assistance, because the paths of life are too dangerous to walk alone.

Prayer. It doesn't have to be long. It doesn't have to be flowery. But it should contain the elements Jesus told us about when he said, "This is how you should pray."

MOTTO

The best way to talk to God is to talk His language.

DEBRIEFING

1. When I pray, do I usually think through the elements of prayer, or do I just say what comes to mind? Should I more diligently plan my prayer time?

2. What can I learn from reading Jesus' prayer in John 17?

3. How do I see prayer? Getting from God, communicating with God, worshiping God, or fulfilling an obligation to God?

CALL TO ACTION

1. If I don't have a prayer list already, I will start one. In this prayer list, I will not only list prayer requests, but also the names of those I pray for.

2. If I haven't done so already, I will memorize the Lord's Prayer.

Father God, I honor your name, I pray that your will is done in my life. Please provide today what I need. Forgive me, Lord, and remind me to forgive others. I need your protection from sin and the advances of the devil. I love you, God.

PLANNING DAY

"Be clear-minded and self-controlled so that you can pray" (1 Peter 4:7).

MARCHING ORDERS

FROM POINT MAN
Read: Chapter Six,
pages 147-155

FROM THE BIBLE
Read: 1 Peter 4:1–11

Don't miss the significance of today's Scripture reading:

•Peter admonishes us to have the same attitude as Jesus Christ, who suffered for us. This means that our constant goal is God's will, not the junk the world offers.

•A clear-minded, self-controlled person is better able to pray, Peter says.

•Among the activities of the believer should be offering hospitality, administering grace, speaking the words of Christ. The bottom line is praising God.

THINKING IT THROUGH

One of the buzzwords in the corporate world these days is "purpose statement."

Unlike some buzzwords that seem faddish and useless, this is a good one. From multinational corporations to small businesses, from churches to Christian parachurch ministries, people are coming up with purpose statements. These concise documents keep employees focused on the reason for the company's existence, and they keep everyone involved from getting sidetracked on useless projects.

First Peter 4:1–11 could very well be a purpose statement for men who want to focus their lives on the right goals. Without discounting at all the entirety of the valuable teaching in those verses, one could boil down those twelve verses into this purpose statement:

We will have the same attitude as Jesus, the one who suffered for us. We will live according to God's will, not our own (leaving selfish, sinful living to the pagans, who must account for themselves). We will keep our mind clear and under control, which helps us pray more effectively. We will love others, serve others, and be hospitable. We will be careful to speak God's words and to live in God's strength so that He will be praised and glorified.

A purpose statement like that, with its single-minded goal of living for God and honoring Him, is a tall order. And like any good purpose statement, it requires a plan if it is to be carried out.

Today, let's try something different. Using these pages as a work sheet, and using the planning suggestions we've talked about earlier, begin to develop your plan for spiritual fitness.

A. *Purpose Statement*

We've examined a sample purpose statement from Peter's first epistle. Now do some brainstorming about your mission in life. Then write it down in fifty words or less.

_____

_____

_____

_____

_____

_____

_____

_____

_____

B. *Scriptural Goals*

The Word of God is a huge book, and it is imposing to think of taking it on all at once. Instead of doing that, perhaps it would be best to pick a few shorter passages that you would like to know better. As you choose passages, also think about your study goals. For example, your study goal for 1 Corinthians 13 might be to discover the characteristics of a loving Christian.

Passage   Study Goal

1. _____ _____
2. _____ _____
3. _____ _____
4. _____ _____
5. _____ _____

C. *Appointment Times*

As I mentioned in *Point Man*, my dad set his appointment with God at 5:45 each morning. Pick a time that is least likely to be interrupted by family responsibilities and then begin to build it into your schedule.

I will meet with God at_____each _____.

Now tell your wife and ask her to help you keep that appointment.

D. *Get Assistance*

Once you decide on an area of study for your beginning appointments, visit a Christian bookstore and get a book that will give you additional insight into the Scripture passages you've selected. Also, make sure you have a Bible that you enjoy reading, and consider getting one with built-in study notes.

Shopping list:

1. A notebook (see next section)
2. _____
3. _____

E. *Begin a Journal*

This may seem to be getting overly complicated, but remember, what you are doing is as important to your spiritual growth and your family's well-being as a company's five-year plan is to its health. It is time well-spent to make sure this works.

In the journal, you can track:
1. spiritual victories.
2. biblical insights from your reading.
3. prayer requests.
4. questions.

F. *Choose a Place*

Find a spot in your house where you are comfortable praying aloud, where you have the quiet you need, and where you can meet with God regularly. Equip that spot with the tools that you purchase or already have on hand. Before you begin, consecrate this area of the house to God and ask Him to make it a sanctuary.

MOTTO

If you're too busy to meet with God today, you're too busy.

Lord, I want to meet with you regularly to get to know you better and to build our relationship. Please help me block out the time, and protect me from the obstacles that will come for sure. Teach me from your Word and from the way you work in my life.

YOU TELL ME; I'LL TELL YOU

"When Peter came to Antioch, I opposed him to his face, because he was clearly in the wrong" (Galatians 2:11).

MARCHING ORDERS

FROM POINT MAN
Read: Chapter Six,
pages 150-152

FROM THE BIBLE
Read: Galatians 2:11–21

As you read today's Scripture passage, consider this:

•Paul made his statement without apology. He saw Peter doing wrong, and he let him know about it.

•Peter had acted somewhat hypocritically, and Paul minced no words in telling him that he was wrong.

THINKING IT THROUGH

Men don't need friends.

That's what a lot of guys think.

Oh, we need guys to shoot baskets with. Or to go hunting with. Or to talk about sports with. Or to go to hockey games with. Or to work on the car with.

But to talk with?

Nope. Not necessary. We get in all of our words with the talking we have to do at work — selling mutual funds or going over the books with the accountant. If we're lucky and don't go over our very short gab quota for the day, we'll even have something to say to the wife and kids after we walk through the door besides just, "Hi, Honey. I'm home."

The preceding rationale is the way things used to be. Before men discovered accountability groups. Before men realized that they can often get themselves into huge amounts of trouble by being secretive and close-mouthed about their spiritual life. Before they realized that God does not save them to be lone rangers, riding the range by themselves.

With the rise of movements like Promise Keepers and with the advent of small group Bible studies, men are discovering that it is now okay to get together with a few buddies and talk about something other than Troy Aikman, Rush Limbaugh, and four-wheelers.

Men are waking up to the realization that it is okay to speak up in a small group talking about God, faithfulness, spiritual service, or how to understand the book of Philippians.

And men are taking this thing even farther. With the growing trend toward accountability groups, guys are beginning to do the Paul-Peter thing. They are beginning to get in each other's face about matters of the heart. Deep conversations are no longer restricted to, "Hey, did you see Sportscenter last night?" They now include questions such as:

"Have you been praying faithfully?"

"What does your spiritual journal say for yesterday?"

"What did God teach you from His Word this morning?"

"When you went on that business trip, did you have HBO in your motel TV room?"

"How much time have you spent with your children in the past week — time that was not interrupted by TV, work, or hobbies?"

"I heard the language you used on the basketball court last Saturday. Do you think that is honoring to God?"

"Your new administrative assistant is very pretty. Have you introduced her to your wife? And are you keeping your eyes where they belong when you're with that new assistant?"

Nosy questions, to be sure. But questions that keep a friend in check — that keep a man from thinking that he can have an unrestrained private thought life or that he can get away with little or no spiritual training.

Notice how forthright Paul was with Peter. "When Peter came to Antioch, I opposed him to his face, because he was clearly in the wrong." That is a tough, courageous, dangerous thing to do. Suppose Peter had taken this advice wrong and had been offended. What would that have done to the cause of Christ?

But worse, what would have happened had Paul not set the record straight for Peter? Peter would have continued to play the hypocrite. He would have done even more damage to the advancement of the gospel.

Think about the concept of accountability like this:

Imagine how things would be different in the Christian community if certain people in the past fifteen years had been kept accountable for their lives on a daily or weekly basis.

We've all heard the stories of once godly preachers who fell into illicit relationships with women. And leaders in the church who got involved in illegal money schemes. And members by the hundreds who drifted away from matters of faith simply because no one ever talked with them about spiritual matters; when they drifted off, no one even noticed.

If we could add up the numbers of people lost to the church the past fifteen years, we would be staggered. Perhaps each of these situations could have been salvaged had the people involved been plugged into an accountability group — if they had not been allowed to drift off spiritually but had instead been kept honest in their relationship with God.

We have too many secrets in the Christian life — too many things we hide from each other while God is grieved. Accountability groups can shine the light of love and God's Word on those secrets, saving us from all kinds of difficulties.

Peter was accountable to Paul, and it may have saved his ministry. To whom are you accountable?

MOTTO

If no one helps us keep on track, we easily become derailed.

DEBRIEFING

1. Do I have an accountability partner? If so, how is it working? If not, why not?

2. How can I also enlist the help of my wife as an open, honest accountability partner?

3. What are some guidelines I need to use so that I don't become obnoxious?

CALL TO ACTION

1. If I don't already have an accountability partner, I will ask _____ to meet with me once a week to check up on things.

2. What areas of my life will benefit by having a partner ask me questions?

a. _____

b. _____

c. _____

Lord, please lead me to the right kind of friend, someone who cares enough for me to ask the tough questions. Then direct my life in a way that helps me pass the accountability that I will have with my friend. Please keep me accountable for my actions and my relationship with you.

A TEAMWORK COUPLE

""Greet Priscilla and Aquila, my fellow workers in Christ Jesus" (Romans 16:3).

MARCHING ORDERS

FROM POINT MAN
Read: Chapter Seven,
pages 157-168

FROM THE BIBLE
Read: Acts 18:1–4,
18–26

In today's brief Bible reading, don't miss these points:

• Exiled from Rome, Aquila and Priscilla settled in Corinth, where they met Paul on his missionary journeys.

• The husband-wife tent-making team shared that occupation with Paul, and they even set up a cooperative venture.

• Later, the three of them sailed to Ephesus, where Paul left the couple to continue the work.

• Aquila and Priscilla took the opportunity to witness to a well-known seeker named Apollos.

THINKING IT THROUGH

Long before Steve and Annie Chapman, Bill and Gloria Gaither, Jack and Rexella Van Impe, or Billy and Ruth Graham, there was Aquila and Priscilla.

They aren't the most often-mentioned couple in the Bible — they don't compete with the Abrahams and Sarahs in scriptural ink. But for a couple in which neither partner was a major player on the stage of Scripture, they are honored with quite a few Bible mentions.

Their status in the pantheon of Bible characters should cause us to wonder what traits they displayed to draw so much attention.

As we look at their role in Paul's life, several characteristics stand out.

First, they survived a crisis. Throughout history we see the mistreatment of certain ethnic groups, and wonder how people can survive such inhumanities. Aquila and Priscilla found themselves in the middle of Claudius' ethnic cleansing of Rome and were forced to flee. We don't know exactly how they handled this crisis, but we do know that they were able to look past it and keep their marriage intact. Good crisis management is one of the signs of a strong marriage.

Second, they seem to be seen as a unit. Some modern thinking about marriage seems to discount the value of seeing a husband and wife as a unit. Each time one is mentioned in Scripture, however, the other is mentioned also. The writers of Scripture also portrayed them together.

Third, they practiced hospitality. Once Aquila and Priscilla got to know Paul, the relationship cemented quickly. One indicator is that Aquila and Priscilla opened their home to Paul for him to stay. A congregation also met at their house (1 Corinthians 16:19). Couples that are not vulnerable usually possess a peaceful home where God is honored.

Fourth, they worked together. Relax, this is not a biblical principle — just an observation. It is often difficult for husbands and wives, who already share so much of life and themselves, to share a job. But these two did — a small business that could have been called A & P Tents.

Fifth, they taught about Jesus Christ. When a Jewish man named Apollos began speaking about Jesus with a limited knowledge of him, Aquila and Priscilla made a special effort to take Apollos aside and instruct him "more adequately" about who Jesus was and all he had done. As a result, Apollos became a key debater when Christians and Jews exchanged ideas.

Sixth, they risked their lives for Paul. This unusual characteristic was mentioned by Paul in Romans 16:4 as he expressed his gratitude for the couple. Jesus had previously said, "Greater love has no one than this, that he lay down his life for his friends" (John 15:13). Truly this couple was unified in their incredible love for their friend Paul.

The example of these two exiled citizens of Rome stands out clearly as a pattern of teamwork. Surely their unselfish service for God and for fellow believers is a clear picture of the kind of marriage that God envisioned in the Garden of Eden when He made Adam and then fashioned a complement for him in Eve.

A couple who work so closely and caringly in unison demonstrates how husbands and wives should cooperate.

Our world often sends husbands and wives off in opposite directions. He is immersed in his occupation, his hobbies, his recreations, even his ministry. She is immersed in her work, her friends, her children, and her ministry. Like twin roller coasters that hit the peaks and valleys on parallel tracks that never cross, they see each other come and go without truly experiencing life together.

How much better the ride is when a husband and wife share the same car on the roller coaster of life. They can enjoy the same high points and battle through the same valleys, always leaning on each other for help.

Taking a cue from Aquila and Priscilla, check out your own life with your wife.

Look at the most recent crisis that visited your home. Did it bring you together or push you apart? We don't know the details about how Aquila and Priscilla handled their exile, but they seemed to come out of it with a stronger marriage. When a crisis appears on the horizon, open up to your wife, offer to help her, ask her for her help, and pray for God's guidance.

One young couple faced a difficult time because of the husband's deteriorating hip. Athletically active and a varsity coach, he faced the prospect of having a hip replacement while in his early thirties. The future had dark clouds ahead, but his wife commented, "The trouble we are having draws us closer to God, and we know that we can be happy only when that happens." Their mutual trust in God led them to a positive consequence of a bad circumstance: A growing relationship with God.

Is the life you share with your wife a unified effort? Is your family one that demonstrates the love of Christ through hospitality or some other service opportunity? Are you together in your zeal to share the good news?

Those are traits of a real teamwork couple. They mark the lives of a man and a woman who have dedicated their lives to a mutual love for God.

MOTTO

A man can have no better friend than a wife who
shares his love, his faith, and his life.

DEBRIEFING

1. What would I say are the three traits I love the most about my wife? Does she know I appreciate her for those things?

2. In the past couple of weeks, have I spent more time doing things with my wife or doing things with others?

3. What three things do we do together as husband and wife that make our life together more enjoyable?

CALL TO ACTION

1. For the next five days, I will remind my wife how thankful I am for these things about her:

a. _____

b. _____

c. _____

2. If I have an accountability partner, I will ask him how he perceives my relationship with my wife. Does he see us as a unit that works together? Does he see me as a loving, kind, caring husband in word and deed?

3. Together, my wife and I will tackle one of these activities together over the next month:

a. _____

b. _____

c. _____

Dear Lord, thank you for my wife. Thank you for her contributions to my life. Please help me to be someone she can depend on to be helpful to her, to lift her up, and to make her feel special. Help us together to be the kind of couple to whom others can look for a good example.

WHEN A MAN LOVES A WOMAN

"Husbands, in the same way be considerate as you live with your wives, and treat them with respect. . ." (1 Peter 3:7).

MARCHING ORDERS

FROM POINT MAN
Read: Chapter Seven,
pages 168-171

FROM THE BIBLE
Read: 1 Peter 3:1–12

Don't miss the significance of today's Scripture reading:

•The first part of 1 Peter 3 speaks to the wife, telling her what is expected of her.

•The example of Sarah is instructive, because she and Abraham faced their share of difficulties, some brought on by Abraham himself.

•Husbands are given specific guidelines in verse 7 about how to interact with their wives.

THINKING IT THROUGH

Charles and Diana. Donald and Ivana. Didn't it look like they loved each other? Didn't it seem that when they looked at each other, it was the genuine article?

Looks can be deceiving. And as these beautiful people found out, looks aren't everything.

When a man loves a woman, it's more than a look. It's more than her looks. It's a commitment of heart, soul, will, and attitude.

It's a dedication to the good of the other person.

As you read this page, think about your wife. Have you sold out your heart to her? Is it your desire to seek her happiness — even at the expense of something you value? Is valuing her more important to you than any other person or thing?

When a man truly loves a woman, it shows.

It showed when Jeff Gordon, upon accepting the 1995 NASCAR championship, acknowledged in tears the vital part his wife Brooke played in his success.

It shows when a pastor stands before his church and speaks only in the most endearing and honest terms about his wife — never using her as a butt of his jokes.

It showed when Bill McCartney stepped down as head coach of the Colorado Buffaloes football team to make sure his wife Lyndi knows he cares for her more than anything.

It shows when a man cancels a business trip because his wife needs him at home more than she needs him to earn a few more dollars.

It showed when a pro football player decided to face the wrath of his coach and pay a huge monetary fine to miss a football game so he could be with his wife during childbirth.

It shows in the everyday husband who gallantly goes to work each day to a job he'd rather quit, works hard at it, and comes home faithfully each night to assist his wife with her work, with the household duties, and with the children.

It shows. And it pays big dividends.

In 1 Peter 3, Peter spells out several vital principles for wife and husband. Since this book talks to guys, let's skip down to verse 7 and see what he has to tell us.

1. *Be considerate.* Frankly, men, we are not noted for this. A lot of women see us as gut-showing, remote-controlling, couch-anchoring slobs who only know how to grunt instructions to the Mrs. and shoo the kids out of the room so we don't miss the third period of another 2-1 hockey game.

That's hardly a good way to demonstrate love.

When a man loves a woman, it shows through considerate behavior. *Tenderness* when a woman faces a crisis. *Compassion* when she isn't feeling well. *Understanding* when you don't see eye to eye.

2. *Treat her with respect.* A nationally known preacher stood before a crowd of two thousand people and made the following insensitive remark. "After being married for all these years, I looked over at my wife one morning and said, 'What happened to you?'" Actually, the same thing happened to her that happened to him. They both got old.

What insensitivity!

To respect the special woman you married means to always put her in the best possible light; to ensure that others see her as the most special woman in your world; to make her feel as special now as she was the day you married her.

3. *Understand your partnership.* Believing partners share something no other couple can share: dual faith in Jesus Christ. As 1 Peter 3:7 says, your wife is an heir with you "of the gracious gift of life." There can be no more important tie that binds you together, and your mutual prayers together are an indication of how effective your life together can be.

There is something special about a true love story. Our heartstrings are tugged when we see a man and a woman whose lives are intertwined with a loving, caring bond.

God's design for marriage leaves plenty of room for that kind of heartwarming relationship. A man whose life is marked by a spirit that forgives, a heart that is tender, a passion for protection, and a tongue that is kind will find himself honoring God in his relationship with his wife.

What do people say when you and your wife's names are mentioned? Do they see two people in love who are dedicated to serving God? Do they see kindness and admiration, coupled with mutual respect?

If they do, they know they've seen a man who loves a woman. After all, it shows.

*Your love for your wife shines beyond your home; it
brightens many people's lives.*

DEBRIEFING

1. Do I think that most of the conflicts that arise in our home are my fault or my wife's? With the problems that are my fault, could I have avoided some of them with more consideration and respect?

2. How have I demonstrated my love to my wife in the past week? How have I demonstrated my concern for her well-being?

CALL TO ACTION

1. I will make an effort to pray more often with my wife.

2. Each day this next week I will make an effort to show my wife I love her in a special way. Following are some ideas I can put to use:

a. _____

b. _____

c. _____

d. _____

Dear heavenly Father, please guide my actions and my attitude toward my wife. Help me to be tender and considerate of her. Thank you for giving her to me. Help my love for her show to others.

AN OUT-OF-CONTROL COUPLE

"Take care of that cursed woman..." (2 Kings 9:34).

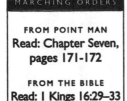

MARCHING ORDERS

FROM POINT MAN
Read: Chapter Seven,
pages 171-172

FROM THE BIBLE
Read: I Kings 16:29–33

As you read today's Scripture passage, consider this:

•Ahab's evil heart prompted him to marry an evil woman.

•Jezebel threatened one of God's top people, Elijah.

•The evil of Ahab and Jezebel, in tandem, led to Naboth's murder.

•Jezebel's gruesome death was a fitting punishment for a wicked life.

THINKING IT THROUGH

And we think the royal family in England is in trouble. Ahab and Jezebel make the House of Windsor look like a fairy tale.

This sixth century B.C. royal family was evil from the word go. According to the Bible, Ahab "did more evil in the eyes of the Lord than any of those before him" (1 Kings 16:33).

Ahab followed in the evil footsteps of Jeroboam, who had set up idols for worship. Ahab also married Jezebel, an equally wicked woman.

Together, these two left a legacy of hatred for the things of God.

Among the evil deeds of Jezebel: she had God's prophets killed (1 Kings 18:4), she threatened Elijah's life (19:1–2), and she had Naboth killed for his vineyards (21:1–16).

Ahab and Jezebel were an out-of-control couple.

On a less deadly scale, any couple that does not base its marriage on the solid, unchanging instructions in God's Word is likewise out of control.

Evil does not limit its visits to people as bad as these two. It can work its destructive ways in couples even when both partners claim to know Jesus as Savior.

Some of Ahab and Jezebel's traits can get us in trouble in our own marriages:

1. *Not learning from the mistakes of our predecessors.* Ahab should have learned from Jeroboam that idolatry was wrong, but he embraced false gods anyway. Likewise, when we emulate the mistakes of people we know who think their ways are better than God's, we're asking for trouble.

2. *Failing to make God the center of our worship.* In the case of Ahab and Jezebel, their object of worship was Baal. In our homes, the problem could be materialism, or entertainment, or sports, or anything else that attracts more attention, time, and energy than God.

3. *Letting greed and covetousness cause us to make dumb decisions.* Of course, we are not going to cause the death of someone to get his land, but we may do untold damage to our families if we work so hard to accumulate cars, homes, real estate, and other things that we neglect them. An out-of-control couple constantly searches for earthly possessions at the expense of eternal rewards.

4. *Ignoring the possible consequences of our actions.* The fear of God, we are told in Proverbs, is the beginning of wisdom. It is good, then, to have a healthy respect for God and an understanding that He has the right as our Father to punish us for our wrongdoing. A couple who share this right-thinking fear of God

will never allow themselves to entertain thoughts of sinful behavior that could lead to the breakup of their marriage. Too many times, a spouse will go ahead with a sin that threatens his or her marriage, simply because he or she did not fear the consequences God may have for that behavior (see 2 Kings 9:30–37).

So many factors in life are beyond our control. We often have little to do with what jobs we get and which we lose. Try as we might, we cannot always control how our children respond to our spiritual teaching. We certainly cannot control how others respond to us.

But we can control ourselves. As Christian men, we don't have to live out-of-control lives. By depending on the help of the Holy Spirit, we can avoid the temptations that can threaten us, we can control how well we treat our wives, we can keep our minds focused on what will enhance our relationship.

If our spouses also allow the Spirit to control their lives, we can rest assured that despite the problems that will come, we never have to be an out-of-control couple.

The difference between Aquila and Priscilla and Ahab and Jezebel is a gulf of insurmountable distance. Let's follow the example of the former couple, whose control led them to be such a tremendous help to Paul.

No one will ever immortalize us in Scripture, but our family will notice the difference and thank God for us.

MOTTO

A couple that lives under God's control will be successful in God's work.

DEBRIEFING

1. How much of my life do I try to control by my own intellect and savvy, and how much do I let God control?

2. Obviously I'm not as bad as Ahab and my wife is no Jezebel, but in what areas do we need to establish more spiritual discipline?

3. If someone were to write a description of my wife and me in a book for posterity, what would it say?

1. My wife and I will review our vows to each other and rededicate ourselves to letting God have control over problem areas in our lives.

2. I'm trying to control these three areas of my life and now will turn them over to God:

a. _____

b. _____

c. _____

Lord, please take my marriage and control it. Lead me to treat my wife as I should. Help me to be controlled by your Spirit in those areas that are problems for me right now. Thank you for my wife. Help me to cherish her and help her to be the woman you want her to be.

JESUS AND ME?

"Husbands, love your wives, just as Christ loved the church..." (Ephesians 5:25) *for "the Son of Man did not come to be served, but to serve..."* (Mark 10:45).

MARCHING ORDERS

FROM POINT MAN
Read: Chapter Seven, pages 173-183

FROM THE BIBLE
Read: Ephesians 5

Meditate on today's Bible passage:

•Notice the first thing we read about Jesus in Ephesians 5 is that "Christ loved us and gave Himself up for us..." (verse 2).

•Think about the actions considered off limits in verses 3–14. Consider how demonstrating Christlike selflessness helps us avoid these traps.

•Introducing the family section of this chapter with a call to "submit to one another," Paul sets the tone for successful family living.

•Through the rest of this passage, observe how carefully Paul weaves in the importance of following Christ's example.

THINKING IT THROUGH

Are you a Promise Keeper?

The past few years this movement has been sweeping the country, calling men everywhere to a new awareness of their biblical role in the family.

As thrilling as this phenomenon is to men who want a revival of Christian values and godly living in our land, though, it has not been met with universal acceptance.

Some people look at the Promise Keeper call for the man to take on a leadership role in the home and immediately conjure up images of a caveman grabbing his woman by the hair and dragging her back to their little house on the mountain. They think a man who wants to be the head of his house is the worst thing since Ozzie Nelson.

If it weren't such a serious subject, this misconception would be funny, for it drips of irony. The twist is that the biblical call for family leadership by the male is the absolutely safest, most honoring, most loving, and most respectful situation a man and woman can find themselves in. Yet those who don't understand it are afraid of it.

Do you understand it?

What do you think of when you read, "Wives, submit to your husbands as to the Lord"? Do you see an opening to push "the little woman" all over the house? Do you see it as a way to keep your wife in the kitchen? Do you see it as a way to make sure you get to choose what to watch on TV? Do you see it as your answer to the burning question, "How can I spend more time with the guys?"?

Or do you see it as perhaps the biggest responsibility you will ever have?

That's what it is, and here's why.

When Paul wrote those words, he was putting them in a context that is as challenging as anything you'll ever experience. He was suggesting that the wife is to submit to a husband who is like Jesus.

Now we're talking challenging.

Jesus, who told us in crystal-clear terms that he didn't come to earth so people could wait on him like he was some visiting potentate. He came here to serve us (Mark 10:45).

Jesus, who stood there in the garden and let Roman soldiers arrest him even though he had done nothing wrong.

Jesus, who calmly listened to abusive accusers and their trumped-up charges — without as much as a brief rebuttal.

Jesus, who let people make fun of him, beat him, pull out his beard, and kill him in the worst way imaginable — all the time holding at bay the power that created the universe.

How that Man conducts himself as the Husband of the Church is how we should conduct ourselves as the leaders in our homes.

Look at some other examples in Jesus' life, examples that seem almost domestic in their implications, revealing to us in real-life terms how Jesus served others.

In one incident during Jesus' stay on earth, the disciples had been fishing all night. When they came ashore, Jesus greeted them and offered them a breakfast of fish that he prepared. Indeed, Jesus, the King of the Universe, was not above rustling up some food for his friends (John 21:10–14).

Another time, in a more well-known incident, Jesus was meeting with his disciples in the Upper Room (see John 13). It was the meal that would become known as the Last Supper. In a gesture of servanthood that stands out because of its implications, Jesus washed the disciples' feet. This was a job normally reserved for household servants, so Jesus' willingness to do it demonstrated his heart of service.

In the middle of another trying time for Jesus — right after some Pharisees had come to test him with a tough question — a group of children were brought to Jesus. Thinking that their friend would not want to be bothered, the disciples rebuked the people who brought them. Jesus would have none of that. He asked that the children be brought to him and he blessed them. Jesus, who fought the press of huge crowds wherever he went and who was pressured by questions meant to trip him up, took time out to honor children.

In each of these incidents, Jesus set aside his glory as the Master of all of the earth so he could serve. That is true servant-leadership. He remained the head and the authority, but he never let that leadership stop him from serving others. That's how much Christ loved the church.

Likewise, how much we love our wife is indicated by how willing we are to serve her. Not demand of her. Not use her. Not abuse her. But serve her.

A man with a servant heart shows he loves his wife. A man with a demanding, my-way-or-the-highway heart shows he loves himself.

Let's examine our relationship with the woman we worked so hard to woo and to win not so long ago. We served her then by romancing her and demonstrating our love unselfishly. We need to serve her now in the same way. The Jesus way.

MOTTO

Follow Jesus Christ's example: Love your wife the way he loves you.

DEBRIEFING

1. What have I done in the past week for my wife that demonstrated I am looking out for her welfare before I look out for mine?

2. What frightens me about this idea of Christlike servant-leadership? Am I afraid I won't be perceived as manly or a leader? If so, what does that mean I think about Jesus Christ — the one who washed his disciples' dirty feet — as a leader?

3. What does my wife think of my leadership style? Perhaps I need to ask her if I am serving her.

CALL TO ACTION

1. In my journal this week, I will chart my relationship with my wife by finishing these statements:

a. I demonstrated servant-leadership when I _____
_____. My wife responded
to that by _____.
b. I tried to push my weight around when I _____
_____. My wife
responded to that by _____.

2. In these four areas, I will be more Christlike, demonstrating servanthood rather than selfishness:

a. _____
b. _____
c. _____
d. _____

Dear Lord, thank you for my wife. Please help me to be a servant-leader, following Jesus' example. Help me to think of her needs first, rather than my own. Help me to be sensitive to what is on her heart. Give me strength to overcome bad habits in this regard so I can honor you in my marriage.

THE BABY PROBLEM

"All the days ordained for me were written in your
book before one of them came to be" (Psalm 139:16).

MARCHING ORDERS

FROM POINT MAN
Read: Chapter Eight,
pages 185-197

FROM THE BIBLE
Read: Psalm 139:1–16

In today's brief Bible reading, don't miss these points:

•God knows each person completely. Even more remarkable, God knows each person's life before he or she is even born.

•Children are not a commodity adults can choose to ignore or take care of. Each is a God-ordained life, full of potential and value.

THINKING IT THROUGH

Remember that great 1994 World Series? The remarkable pitching. The clutch hitting. The excited fans cheering the winning team during that thrilling seventh game? Recall that bottom-of-the-ninth grand slam home run to... What is that, you say? There was no 1994 World Series?

Indeed, there wasn't. Whether you like baseball or not, you probably know how much the game of baseball was hurt by the fact that part of a season and an entire post-season were wiped out. Although all the games were scheduled, not all were played. Greed wiped them out.

That's pretty sad. But it is nothing compared to another kind of cancellation taking place in our society.

Lives of children — pre-ordained lives that God had already put a special mark on — are being wiped out by the millions. Abortion, we call it. And each such act takes a life that God had planned and reduces it to "what would have been."

Missing the 1994 World Series was irritating. Missing the millions and millions of children who have been obliterated since 1973 is heart-wrenching.

Psalm 139 makes it clear that each life God creates is designed for a purpose, designed with a plan, and designed with love. To arbitrarily decide a little life is not valuable and throw away God's plan is symptomatic of a society that does not value children.

•Abortionists exploit unborn children by making money off their demise.

•Equally horrible, child pornographers rob children of their innocence to fill their bank accounts.

•Advertisers often prey on the immaturity of children by manipulating them to want their products — whether the products are helpful or not.

•TV and movie producers continue to lower their standards, without consideration of how children are affected.

•Young couples increasingly decide not to have children because they don't want their lifestyles cramped by the 24-hour-a-day responsibilities of diapers, strollers, and baby-sitters.

Clearly, our society is in many ways anti-children.

Our affluent civilization has been able to create items that seem to have more value than children. We have cars that cost $30,000 and need to be babied. We have homes that are palatial and need to be protected from kid-damage. Children appear far down the list of possible blessings this life has to offer.

No matter how poorly our world treats children, though, we know that each one is "fearfully and wonderfully made." Each child has intrinsic value that doesn't depend on performance or looks.

As men — as dads — then, our mission from God is to mirror His love for children whenever we can. The God who created each child is honored when we show love and respect for the little ones of the world — and especially the ones He has entrusted specifically to us.

How do we go about changing the world for our children, letting them know that they are special to us simply because they are God-created and God-loved?

1. Treat them with the respect they deserve as God's special people.

2. Maintain a strong, daily relationship with them by nurturing their heart with love and concern.

3. Demonstrate a genuine appreciation of the them by spending time each day seeing how God's plan for that part of their life was carried out.

4. Provide for their needs while teaching that those provisions are from God.

5. Introduce them to God and instruct them in righteousness.

6. Value them far more than any possession, job, or outside relationship.

Remember, though, that it is not just the children God has given you who need help. Because society at large does not value children, men and women of faith must step forward and demonstrate their value.

1. Support those who are working with children in such ventures as orphanages, relief organizations, and ministries to children of prisoners.

2. Consider taking in a foster child if God has blessed you with the necessary spiritual, physical, and emotional resources.

3. Befriend your children's friends and make a positive impact on them.

4. Do what you can to educate people about the atrocities of abortion.

If we want to weigh the value of some blessing from God's perspective, perhaps we should do so by considering how often He bestows that blessing. For instance, because God continually answered the prayers of the great churchman and friend of children of eighteenth century England, George Mueller, isn't that a sure sign of God's hand of blessing?

Think of that in regard to children. God has bestowed on this earth children by the billions. If we think of each birth as another gift from God's hands, imagine how blessed this world is.

And imagine how it pleases God's heart when we do all we can to take care of children.

MOTTO

The greatest test of godly love in our heart is how we treat children.

DEBRIEFING

1. In what ways do I sometimes find children more an irritant than a blessing?

2. In what ways have I contributed to the well-being of children other than my own?

3. If someone were to rate me in my love for children, would that person say I love them, tolerate them, or can't stand them?

CALL TO ACTION

1. In the next week, I will set aside at least _____ a day to do stuff with my kids.

2. Each day do I:
   a. hug my children?
   b. pray with my children?
   c. pray for my children?

d. tell them "I love you"?

e. compliment my children?

f. help my children?

g. show my children I love their mother?

h. tuck them in bed?

3. What will I do to help several children who don't have the resources my kids have?

Dear heavenly Father, thank you for being my Father and for showing me your love in so many ways. Please strengthen me, Lord, as I try to be a good father. Instruct me in the way I should treat my children. Help me model Jesus Christ for them every day. Show me how to help other children too.

TWO GREAT GIFTS

"Sons are a heritage from the Lord, children a reward from him" (Psalm 127:3).

MARCHING ORDERS

FROM POINT MAN
Read: Chapter Eight,
pages 196-197

FROM THE BIBLE
Read: Psalms 127–128

Compare today's Scripture reading with these related passages:

•According to Genesis 33:1–5, children are a direct gift from God.

•According to Romans 6:23, another gift God gives is salvation — the greatest gift of all.

THINKING IT THROUGH

Do you love to be around people who give gifts? Who doesn't? Some men and women find great joy in giving to others.

• Many churches have enjoyed the blessing of a "candy man" — perhaps a grandpa or someone else who buys candy and distributes it each Sunday to the children of the church. He's happy because he is giving, and the children flock to him to make sure he has plenty of opportunities to exercise his gift.

• Many communities benefit from the philanthropy of local citizens who donate large sums of money to help civic projects. Nobody is forcing these people to give; they love to put some of their extra money back into their hometown.

- Many parents spend their lives in service to their children, sharing what is most important with their sons and daughters — themselves.

- Many Christian and other nonprofit organizations benefit from volunteers who freely give their time and expertise to help get everything done.

We enjoy being around these kind of people. They are easy to like because they have a genuine concern for others — a concern that leads to their giving important resources to help others.

One of the greatest gift-giving stories in literature, written by O. Henry, is called "The Gift of the Magi." In this story, set at Christmastime, a young couple grieve because they are too poor to buy each other presents for the holiday. (You can't write a story like that today; the modern couple would simply pull out a credit card and go for it.)

Despite their poverty, both the husband and wife in O. Henry's story use ingenuity and self-sacrifice to give something to the other. The wife, unable to find the cash she needs to purchase the gold chain she wants so badly to buy for his watch, sells her hair to get the money.

Lovingly, carefully, and with satisfaction, she prepares to give her husband the gold chain.

Likewise, the husband is out hunting for a perfect gift for her. He finally finds it and prepares to purchase it. To raise the needed cash, he too sells a very important item.

The time comes to exchange their presents.

Imagine the shock when the wife, newly shorn, opens her brand-new set of hair combs.

Imagine the shock when the husband, newly bereft of the watch he sold to buy her combs, finds she has purchased a gold chain.

It is the quintessential story of love finding its best expression in giving what is most important to honor someone dear. The giving of gifts, as this story implies, is the ultimate in demonstrative love.

No person, however, can give gifts like God can!

Not even the greatest philanthropist can match the greatest gifts God has poured out for us. And not even the greatest self-sacrifice of one human for another can begin to emulate God's greatest gift to us.

God is the grand giver of gifts — the ultimate benefactor.

And the two greatest gifts He has given are life itself and salvation.

When God gives a child to a couple — whether through natural processes or through adoption — He has worked one of the greatest miracles we know of this side of heaven.

If you are a dad, think about that child God has placed in your care. He or she is an eternal being, made to live forever. God created that child through a miraculous process, breathed a soul into him or her, and made plans for his or her life. That child has in its power the opportunity to change the world, find a cure for a disease, cause wars to cease, invent new and great innovations. He or she will touch hundreds, thousands, possibly millions of lives in a lifetime.

He or she will bring hours of happiness, teach myriad lessons, and, yes, even cause moments of heartache.

He or she is priceless, unrepeatable, invaluable, and unique.

For those reasons and more, a child is a gift like nothing else God gives. It is our job as the parents of these gifts to make sure they are handled with the same care God would show if He Himself had direct charge of their care.

But as marvelous as children are, they are not God's greatest gift. That is the gift of eternal life.

How ironic that in an era in which people are moving away from God and away from the knowledge of the gift of salvation, they are also moving away from seeing children as a gift from God.

To many, God's salvation through Jesus Christ is just as inconvenient as children. One can be avoided by ostracizing God's people; the other can be avoided by abortion.

How you view these two gifts from God speaks volumes about your relationship with Him.

What an awesome God we have! He has given us the two greatest gifts we could ever imagine: children and eternal life. Let's praise Him forever.

Two things we can take with us to heaven — our salvation and our children.

DEBRIEFING

1. Do I ever grow weary of my children and think of them as anything less than gifts from God? What causes that kind of thinking?

2. What would life be like without either children or salvation? Some people do not want children and do not want salvation. What is their loss?

3. Besides children and salvation, what other great gifts have I received from God? How do they compare with the first two?

CALL TO ACTION

1. I will spend some time in prayer today, thanking God for my children and His free gift of salvation.

2. Another way to thank God for salvation is to share the good news with someone else so he or she can also enjoy this great free gift. So, I will communicate that message to these two people within the next month:

a. _____

b. _____

My dear Creator, thank you for giving me life, for sustaining my life, and for giving my life purpose. And thank you for my children, who are a direct gift from you. Please help me to show appreciation for salvation by spreading the word. Help me to show appreciation for my children by making them the most special people in my life.

LISTEN, MY SON

*"My son, if you accept my words . . . then you will
understand the fear of the Lord. . ."* (Proverbs 2:1,

FROM POINT MAN
Read: Chapter Nine,
pages 199-202

FROM THE BIBLE
Read: Proverbs 2:1-10

Don't miss the significance of today's
Scripture reading:

•Here a father tells his son that the
way to wisdom starts with listening to
him. Of course, Solomon was the wisest
man in the world, so that would help a
bit!

•Wisdom cannot be granted as a gift. A father can teach and
instruct, but wisdom ultimately comes from God.

•Along with wisdom, Solomon also tells about the importance of doing what is right, just, and fair.

THINKING IT THROUGH

Fishing doesn't seem all that complicated, does it? Just drop a
hook in the water and wait for supper to swim by.

Watch a dad teaching his little boy to fish, though, and you
begin to realize how complicated it can be. Learning to fish is a
part of growing up. And dads who are spending a Saturday after-
noon at the lake making sure Junior understands this important
growing up ritual are not about to take the chore lightly.

It starts with a complete explanation of which spots to fish. Then there's the speech about safety and the obligatory story of the time ol' dad sunk a hook into Uncle Ned's scalp. Of course, lessons must be provided on what kind of bait or lure to use, which bobber is best, and the importance of keeping the tackle box well-organized.

And that's not to mention the casting lessons, which may or may not end with Dad fishing the rod and reel out of the water.

Finally, Junior has heard all the instructions and gets to actually drown his first worm. How disheartened Dad is when, after fifteen seconds of waiting, Junior says, (a) I have to go to the bathroom, (b) I'm bored, or (c) can I go ride my bike?

Fishing is one of the hundreds of life skills we dads are called on to teach our sons and daughters. And each new concept, skill, or principle we teach takes time and thought.

The book of Proverbs is all about teaching life skills. It is an instruction book — dad to son — that contains advice on perhaps the most important life skill of all: how to be wise. All the other things we teach our children pale in importance when compared with instructing them in wisdom.

Think about all the sports stars who have excelled at a game someone taught them but lacked the wisdom to handle big league pressures. Think of the successful business people you hear about who have "had it all" yet have been unhappy, simply because they were not wise enough to manage their own lives.

Rich or poor, successful or failing, what will really dictate how a life is lived is wisdom.

So Solomon sets out to instruct his son in wisdom.

As we try to do the same with our sons, perhaps it would be helpful to follow Solomon's advice. In a nutshell, he says to his son:

•*Accept your father's words.* We must earn the respect of our children if we expect them to learn anything more important than fishing from us.

•*Store up your father's commands.* Both now and in the future,

Solomon's advice would help his son. A son often looks back with fondness to pet sayings of his dad, which is a great way to help him store up our thoughts.

•*Listen for wisdom.* We can begin to tune our son's ears toward wisdom by pointing it out and leading him to additional sources that might bring him wisdom.

•*Apply your heart to understanding.* The more we spend time explaining concepts and sharing insights, the more our children will gain a love for understanding.

•*Call out for insight.* If our sons were to call out to us for insight, would we hear? Would we respond? If they get it from us, they'll keep calling.

•*Cry aloud for understanding.* It all depends on keeping open dialogue with him.

•*Understand the fear of the Lord and find the knowledge of God.* How much instruction do we give our little guys on what it means to have a healthy fear of God? How often do we talk about God's awesomeness with them?

It is so natural for us to want to spend time with our kids teaching them the purely fun things in life. It is sometimes tougher to carve out time for spiritual pursuits. But if they are to find hope in a passage like Proverbs 2, they're going to have to know that when they turn to us for help, we'll be there.

Our boys will have many teachers in life. We have to be careful which ones influence our boys the most.

One parent said that she had to take her son out of a school because he had a teacher who was too good. The boy was in second grade, and he had a teacher who was well-liked and respected. Some of his ideas were contradictory, however, with what his family thought was right. When the parents tried to explain that the teacher was wrong, the little boy protested that his teacher was always right.

Serious problems develop if we dads lose the No. 1 spot as a teacher in our boys' lives. If we want them to gain the understanding of God that the Bible alone can give them, we must keep the classroom open at home.

If Solomon can write a whole book on the subject, we can give it some of our time too.

MOTTO

Every dad needs to be his son's favorite teacher.

DEBRIEFING

1. In the past few weeks, what have I been teaching my son in two worlds: the purely educational and the spiritual?

2. How is my child doing in the area of understanding God and loving Him? Do we ever talk God-talk?

3. What have I done recently to help my child become more wise in his decision-making?

CALL TO ACTION

1. In the next few weeks, I will strive to teach my child wisdom in two of the following areas:

    a. money

    b. male/female relationships

    c. godliness

    d. school

    e. friends

2. I will set aside two times in the next week to spend with my son so we can talk about the importance of wisdom.

GOD AND ME

Dear God, thank you for the responsibility of teaching my child. Please help me to search for wisdom so I can teach it to him. Show me how to show him a love for you that is real. Encourage my son toward spiritual pursuits and help me know how to direct him.

A WORD ABOUT
SOMETHING SHAMEFUL

"The wrath of God is being revealed from heaven against all the godlessness and wickedness of men who suppress the truth..." (Romans 1:18).

MARCHING ORDERS

FROM POINT MAN
Read: Chapter Nine,
pages 202-206

FROM THE BIBLE
Read: Romans 1:18–32

As you read today's Scripture passage, consider this:

• People who choose sinful ways neglect to find God, who is discoverable by anyone who wants to find him.

• Those who have been "given over" to their sinful desires participate in things the Scripture calls wicked. Included in that list is this: "Men committed indecent acts with other men..." (Romans 1:27).

• Notice what other evils were spoken of in the same context.

THINKING IT THROUGH

God's Word has spoken clearly on the subject of homosexual activity. Recently, however, the scriptural denunciation of this activity has been questioned, softened, and in many cases, eliminated. How strange that a teaching that had survived for so long has been suddenly judged erroneous.

It's not because of some great new revelation or some scholarly discovery that this teaching has been changed by many, but because a changing culture is forcing a new way of viewing scriptural teaching.

And that changed culture is the one our sons and daughters are growing up in. It's a culture that has turned normalcy on its ear in an effort to break all of the past sexual rules.

In the past thirty years, all of the time-honored standards of sexual behavior have been pummeled by opponents of morality. One short generation ago, the following activities were considered wrong in nearly every segment of society:

- premarital sex

- nudity in cinema

- sexual talk on television

- unmarried couples living together

- homosexual activity

- using sexually-based obscenities in public

Today, those who still consider these wrong are considered aberrations, not normal and moral.

From a culture that based its rules on the authority of Scripture, we have become a culture that either ignores the Bible in these matters or twists the Scripture to make it say what we want.

What else would explain the fact that even people in many churches are going with this new flow?

Although many don't care what the Scripture says about a subject such as homosexual activity, it is our job as dads to instruct our boys and girls. It is our challenge to help them understand why the practice of this sexual sin is so unacceptable.

One way to begin is to make sure they know some of the relevant Scripture passages. Leviticus 18:22 says, "Do not lie with a man as one lies with a woman..." First Corinthians 6:9 says that practicing homosexuals will not inherit the kingdom of God. Jude

7 refers to the homosexual sin that brought down Sodom and Gomorrah (see also Genesis 19).

The onslaught of homosexual instruction that may come your children's way needs also to be countered with God's general teaching on sex. Clearly, God's way is a way of morality, and that morality means that any kind of sexual activity that occurs outside the bounds of marriage is wrong.

Follow this logic and see if it doesn't give you a new way of appreciating how wrong homosexual activity is.

First, consider Hebrews 13:4, which says, "Marriage should be honored by all, and the marriage bed kept pure, for God will judge the adulterer and all the sexually immoral." Here, in very clear language, the inspired author explains that the only acceptable sexual activity is found in marriage. Fornicators (people who engage in sexual activity outside of marriage) and adulterers (people who engage in sexual activity with someone who is already married) are out of God's bounds.

Second, think about what the Scripture teaches about marriage. It is modeled for us with the first couple, Adam and Eve, who joined in this new relationship. Throughout Scripture, whenever marriage is mentioned (and this seems obvious, but needs to be spelled out), it is a male-female relationship.

Any kind of non-marital sexual activity, whether a male and a female, a male and a male, or a female and a female, is outside the bounds of God's plan and therefore wrong. Clearly, if God forbids people of the same sex from engaging in sexual activity, He would not condone what has been called "marriages" between two same-sex partners.

Our children need to know that regardless of how long and how loudly homosexual activists protest, their activity is not acceptable. And they need to know that the biblical teaching is clear.

This topic has been twisted in many ways to make it look presentable. It has been presented as a rights issue, equating it somehow to the plight of African-Americans, whose rights were taken from them because of their race. It has been presented as a loving alternative to heterosexual relations. And it has been championed as something to be taught in our public schools.

This means it's likely that someone will stand before your child and talk about homosexuality in glowing terms. Is he or she ready for such a situation?

Prepare them now, before someone else leads them to a life they will only regret.

MOTTO

In a society that is open to sexual immorality, we need to open the Scripture and talk about morality.

DEBRIEFING

1. What have I told my children about homosexuality? Do I think they know about it or not?

2. What do I think is the best way to explain it to them? How can I explain the immoral nature of it?

3. Why would God be interested in stopping a homosexual activity?

4. What programs or music do my children have access to that could be sending them wrong signals about this topic?

CALL TO ACTION

1. In the next few months, I will read an article or book that explains the homosexual agenda and homosexual activity from a Christian perspective.

2. If this issue has sneaked up on me without my recognizing how the general consensus has changed, I will begin collecting feature articles and news stories that demonstrate what the homosexual agenda is.

Dear God, please help me to have your wisdom when talking with my children about this issue. Protect them from any confusion about their own sexuality. May they grow up to be godly, holy young adults.

THE GOOD, THE BAD, AND THE UGLY

"As for me and my household, we will serve the Lord"
(Joshua 24:15).

MARCHING ORDERS

FROM POINT MAN
Read: Chapter Nine,
pages 206-218

FROM THE BIBLE
Read: I Samuel 2:12–22

As you read today's Bible verses, think about these questions:

•In talking things over with the tribes of Israel, Joshua recognized that some would not agree that serving God is the best option. According to Joshua 24:15, what was his plan of action?

•Another family, Eli's, didn't fare as well. According to 1 Samuel 2:12–22, his sons sinned greatly before God. How did Eli fail in his duties as a father?

THINKING IT THROUGH

It seems like such an easy question.

Are kids better off with a father in the house or not?

Dan Quayle's comments about Murphy Brown several years ago seemed to jump start the discussion, and the debate has escalated since then.

Many recent findings support the theory that it's better to have both mom and dad there for the kids, yet that won't satisfy everyone. In this world where traditions are not sacrosanct anymore, the controversy probably will go on for years.

What is important to us, though, is not who wins the argument. Bad dads can bring about horrendous results.

How many youngsters have been led down the wrong road by a father who indulged a harmful habit, only to watch his children follow in his footsteps?

How many children have been led to believe that they are not important because their dad, though in the home, paid no attention to them?

It's not the presence of the dad that makes the difference, it's how he uses the opportunity. That means that we must not only be there for our children, we must also take actions that will instruct, train, nurture, and support our children.

A couple of passages in the Bible help us understand the difference between a dad who cares enough to put forth the effort and one who has things on his mind other than his children.

First, look at Joshua 24:15. Here Joshua was challenging the people of Israel. They seemed to be waffling in their dedication to God, so Joshua told them that if they didn't want to worship the one true God, they could choose false gods.

Then, as if to set the hook, Joshua told them how he was going to approach this subject with his family. As far as he and his family were concerned, there was no choice but to serve the living Lord. It was a take-charge attitude that suggested real involvement in the spiritual training of the family.

Now move ahead a few pages to 1 Samuel 2. Here we read the sad story of a man who loved God and wanted to serve Him but couldn't transfer his devotion to his sons. We don't know all the reasons for Eli's failures, but we know that he was anything but successful. First Samuel 2:12 says, "Eli's sons were wicked men...."

Perhaps he was burdened with the cares of his position; perhaps he didn't feel comfortable spending time with his sons. We simply don't know.

But we do know that regardless of the reasons, one of the problems was Eli's neglect. In 1 Samuel 3:13, we read of God's judgment against Eli and his sons: "For I told him that I would judge his family forever because of the sin he knew about; his sons made themselves contemptible, and he failed to restrain them." Eli was not man enough to stand up to his sons, finding it easier to become uninvolved in their discipline.

Two different fathers, two different philosophies.

We can find variations of these themes in our families today. As we think about what Joshua and Eli did as dads, we need to use what we know about them as yardsticks, measuring our effectiveness.

First, consider Joshua. "For me and my household, we will serve the Lord." Our first order of business at home is to take care of our own spiritual condition. Just as a coach can't lead a team unless he knows the game, neither can we lead our family spiritually if we neglect spiritual growth in our own life.

Historically, women have been the spiritual leaders in America's families. More often than not, men have stood in the background, too preoccupied with business or recreation to worry about God stuff. Training of children, including spiritual training, was something considered best left to the women, who spent the most time with the little ones anyway.

Joshua suggests differently. First, he says he will serve the Lord, and then he commits his whole family to serving Him. That is a promise that must be backed up with action. It may include:

•leading family devotions.

•initiating spiritual discussions.

•ensuring church attendance and participation.

•getting immersed in the Word individually.

•eliminating distractions that harm spiritual growth.

•modelling Christian service.

If the statement of purpose for a family is what Joshua suggested for his, then Dad — as the CEO — must see that purpose is carried out.

The second step is to avoid the mistakes of Eli. Being a dad is a hands-on job. It can't be something that takes place long-distance. Involvement might mean any of these things:

•helping kids with schoolwork.

•coaching a kids-league sports team.

•rearranging some business appointments to accommodate the kids.

•being a gentle, yet firm disciplinarian.

•maintaining a daily, growing relationship with each child.

There are good dads — like Joshua. There are bad dads — like Eli. And there are ugly dads — who refuse to take any responsibility for their children.

And then there is you. Where do you fall in these dad categories? Are you training your children in God's love because of your own spiritual sensitivity, careful not to neglect your children? Your kids couldn't ask for much more than that.

MOTTO

No dad can succeed without a hands-on approach to the spiritual, cultural, and academic training of his children.

DEBRIEFING

1. What five activities have I engaged in during the past week that demonstrated my desire to train my children spiritually?

a. _____

b. _____

c. _____

d. _____

e. _____

2. What spiritual truths have I learned from Scripture this week that I'd like to pass along to my children?

a. _____

b. _____

c. _____

d. _____

e. _____

3. Would I classify myself as a dad who is

___ Good?

___ Bad?

___ Ugly?

CALL TO ACTION

1. This week, I will incorporate these spiritual disciplines in my family's life:

a. _____

b. _____

c. _____

d. _____

e. _____

2. I tend to neglect my children in these areas:

a. _____

b. _____

c. _____

Here's what I plan to do to correct my errors:

a. _____

b. _____

c. _____

Dear God, thank you so much for entrusting me with my family. Please help me to see my children as a loan from you that I have to take care of before I give them back to you. Give me the strength to pour myself into their lives — both spiritually and physically.

IN CHRIST OR OUT OF LUCK

*"Therefore, there is now no condemnation for those
who are in Christ..."* (Romans 8:1).

MARCHING ORDERS

FROM POINT MAN
Read: Chapter Nine,
pages 218-221

FROM THE BIBLE
Read: Romans 8:1–11

In today's brief Bible reading, don't miss these points:

•Because of Jesus' work on the cross, we have been released from condemnation, which puts us in Christ and sets us free.

•Being set free from the law of sin and death helps us live well, because it prevents us from being bound by our sinful nature.

•This puts us on the road to life and peace since it allows us to have a Spirit-controlled mind.

THINKING IT THROUGH

What are you in?

Are you in a gun club? Are you a member of a political party? Are you in *Who's Who Among Widget Makers?* Are you in your college's alumni association, your kid's high school boosters' club, or a neighborhood association?

Think of all the things you are in.

And think of the privileges you get because you are.

It feels good to be "in" things.

Remember when you were in high school (of course, not everyone considers *that* such a great thing) and you wanted to be a part of the "in" crowd or in the band or in the starting lineup on the basketball team or in the school musical?

When you're in, you win. You get to be a partaker of wonderful privileges others can only dream about.

But do you know what the best thing to be in is?

It's not to be in the President's inner circle of friends.

It's not to be in the Baseball Hall of Fame (though that's pretty high on the list).

It's not even to be in the Marines.

It's to be *in Christ.*

When you're in Jesus Christ, you are *somebody!*

Let's review just a few of the privileges you hold by virtue of being in Christ.

• *You are not condemned* (Romans 8:1). Jesus Christ takes the penalty for our sin and wipes it out. Once condemned to an eternity in hell, a person in Christ is freed to enjoy an eternal life in heaven — in God's presence.

• *You are free* (Romans 8:2). Imagine what it would be like to live under the restrictions of "the law of sin and death." It would mean that you would not have the Holy Spirit's work to keep you from piling up sin after sin, which leads to punishment after punishment. Sin is bondage, and without Christ, sin binds you to utter helplessness.

• *You are part of a bigger group* (Romans 12:5). Talk about joining up with the right group! As a believer, you become a member of the church, which is made up of millions of people — all equipped to do God's work.

• *You are sanctified* (1 Corinthians 1:2). In this world of spiritual dangers and rampant temptation, it is good to know that our position in Christ sets us apart. We don't have to immerse our-selves in the world's slop. We can be shielded from it by the help of the Holy Spirit.

• *You get wisdom from above* (1 Corinthians 1:30). Through God's guidance, we can have the righteousness, holiness, and redemption that keep us out of Satan's range and in fellowship with God.

• *You are made alive* (1 Corinthians 15:22). We need not fear death, although we may not like the idea of it. Through Christ's work, we are made alive for eternity.

• *You are a winner* (2 Corinthians 2:14). Like a World Series champ riding in a parade for the best players on earth, we too have the promise of a victory ride. According to this passage, God leads us in a triumphal procession in Christ. And as God leads us along in triumph, we are enabled to tell others the vital news of salvation.

• *You can understand Scripture* (2 Corinthians 3:14). Ever wonder why some people can read the Bible and not have a clue what it says? Perhaps it's because they have not had the veil of confusion lifted. Only those who are in Christ can read the Bible with understanding.

• *You are a new person* (2 Corinthians 5:17). Without this promise, nothing else much matters. If our salvation did not make us new persons — ones who are no longer bound by old sins — we would be of all men most miserable. If we are not in Christ, we are out of luck, stuck in a futile existence on earth and headed for a godless eternity.

Out of gratitude to God for allowing us to be "in Christ," one of the most important things we can do is to instruct and encour-age our children to live an "in Christ" life. But how? What can dads do to influence our offspring to live "in Christ"?

First, we need to make sure they experience the new birth.

We must set aside special times to talk with them about salvation. We must make the gospel clear and then make sure each child has sincerely trusted Jesus Christ.

Second, we need to teach them the importance of living as God's Word tells them to do. A person who is "in Christ" should live in a way that pleases him.

Third, we can help them learn what the Bible says about being "in Christ." By your own example and Scripture you can demonstrate the value and advantages of an "in Christ" life.

MOTTO

When a person learns to live "in Christ," he rarely finds himself in trouble.

DEBRIEFING

1. How do I know I'm in Christ? If God were to ask me to explain why I should be one of His children, what would I tell Him?

2. What other "in Christ" teachings can I find in Scripture?

3. Whom do I know who is not "in Christ" and still needs to be told how to become a "new creation"?

CALL TO ACTION

1. Sometimes, the best way to explain salvation to someone else is to tell a personal testimony, so I will write out my testimony of faith in Christ.

2. When I think back through the past week, how many times did I demonstrate that I was "in Christ"? What will I do about the times I failed to live as the new creation I am?

Thank you, Father, for all you have given me. Thank you for salvation through faith in Jesus Christ, which gives me so many benefits. Thank you for the privilege of being in Christ. Please help me this week to know how to help others find what I've found through Jesus.

HOMESCHOOLING IS FOR EVERY DAD

"These commandments that I give you today are to be upon your hearts. Impress them on your children" (Deuteronomy 6:6–7).

MARCHING ORDERS

FROM POINT MAN
Read: Chapter Ten,
pages 223-228

FROM THE BIBLE
Read: Deuteronomy 6

Don't miss the significance of today's Scripture reading:

•God's commands and decrees were given to teach the children of Israel to fear the Lord.

•The reward for living by those commands and fearing God is to "enjoy long life."

•For a man to teach what he needs to teach his family, he is expected to use the many teachable moments of home life to do it.

THINKING IT THROUGH

Whatever you think of the growing homeschool phenomenon, one thing is clear: parents who teach their children at home are dedicated.

Lest that statement be misinterpreted, please understand that it does not suggest that parents who don't homeschool aren't dedicated. They too love their children and spend quality and quantity time with them.

Yet we must admit something is different about getting up

every day of the school year and — instead of putting them on the bus — putting your kids to work at the kitchen table. To have to be responsible for their learning — from A to Z — is a daunting task.

More and more, men are taking a hands-on approach in homeschooling families, teaching in their strong areas to help round out the children's education. They are spending time in the home, giving one-on-one instruction to their children.

Although homeschooling as just described is not for every family, there is another kind of homeschooling that is.

Each father must make it his goal to provide spiritual homeschooling for his family.

Oh, we may get some supplemental help from Sunday school or a Christian day school, but the primary responsibility for instructing our children in the things of God falls directly into our laps.

Moses gave us a great example of this in Deuteronomy 6. And he prefaced his instructions in spiritual homeschooling by telling us why it was so important.

The instruction we give our children — and their subsequent acceptance or refusal of the teachings of God's Word — will dictate their happiness in life. We may think we are guaranteeing them happiness by giving them clothes from Eddie Bauer or by helping them develop into a top athlete or by seeing to it that they get great scores on their college entrance exams. But we are not revealing the true secret of happiness unless we teach our children the fear of God as instructed in Deuteronomy 6.

In essence, Deuteronomy gives us both a curriculum and a teaching method. See how you might be able to incorporate these factors in the spiritual homeschooling of your family.

A. CURRICULUM

• The commands and laws the Lord has given (see Deuteronomy 5).

• The importance of demonstrating a right fear of the Lord by keeping those commands and laws.

• The value of obeying God.

• God is a single, all-powerful God.

• What it means to love God with one's whole heart, soul, and strength.

• Understanding God's hand at work.

B. TEACHING METHOD

• Impress the laws and commands on your children.

• Talk about those laws and commands in every area of family life.

• Keep those laws and commands close at hand and on your mind at all times.

• Make them evident at all times.

• Review all that God has done for you.

This method of instruction existed in a far different day than ours. In a primarily agricultural society, fathers were home with their children more, and children were with their fathers as they worked side-by-side.

Today, dads generally leave the house in the morning and are gone till supper time. Then they have to do myriad other chores that take them away from the children. They serve on boards, they coach sports teams, they work second jobs, they have recreational interests. When the day is done, a dad often looks back on the day in surprise when he notices that he has spent little or no time with his children.

To homeschool our kids in spiritual things, we must rearrange our priorities to buy more time with them.

Also, we must capitalize on teachable moments. When we hop in the car to run an errand, grab a kid to take along. Then we can attempt to turn the conversation to matters of the Spirit.

And when the down-times come, giving us the rare chance to actually spend time at home, we have to discipline ourselves not to rush for the remote control or the newspaper or the computer. We must instead rush for the children and look for new ways to influence them toward godliness.

The Old Testament makes it clear that passing down the faith from generation to generation is important. Family lines are essential in the biblical economy. And today, they seem even more so. We must see it as our mission to get the next troops in the battle ready.

We must train our children to be the kind of Christian soldiers who can help the faith move onward. And if it takes giving up some free time to homeschool our children in the things of God, we need to make the sacrifice.

Of all the curricula in the world of education, none compares with what Moses told the families of Israel to observe.

Let's make sure it is part of our home teaching curriculum, as well. Anything less would be a failure.

MOTTO

We can never teach our children too much about God,
but we most often teach them too little.

DEBRIEFING

1. What specific biblical principles have I taught my children in the past month?

2. In the past week, how much time did I spend with my children? How much of that time was spent teaching the "laws and commands" of God?

3. My passion for my children in regard to spiritual things is that they learn _____
_____.

1. I will teach these three biblical principles to my children in the next week:

a. _____

b. _____

c. _____

2. Moses talked about a 24-hour-a-day instructional plan. What are some situations in which I will give my children the spiritual training they need?

Lord, please help me clear my schedule so I can spend more time with my children. Teach me how to carve teachable moments out of each day so I can share with my children truths from Scripture. Help me to make spiritual training an everyday, all-day occurrence at my house.

CAUTION: WOMEN AT WORK

"My son, pay attention to my wisdom, listen well to my words of insight, that you may maintain discretion and your lips may preserve knowledge" (Proverbs 5:1–2).

MARCHING ORDERS

FROM POINT MAN
Read: Chapter Ten,
pages 228-235

FROM THE BIBLE
Read: Proverbs 5

As you read today's Scripture passage, consider this:

• Solomon had to establish his authority and his personal concern for his son before he could begin to instruct him.

• An adulteress doesn't care about what she is doing to harm other people.

• Solomon made it clear that staying far away from an immoral woman was the only way to stay free from her grasp.

• The painful results of sexual sin are lifelong.

• God has a clear view of our actions.

THINKING IT THROUGH

The politically correct police would have a field day with Proverbs 5. They would blow the whistle on Solomon because of his one-sided view. His instructions to his son would be viewed as anti-feminine.

Yet, Solomon wasn't concerned about all that. He was concerned about his son, and he wanted to tell him how dangerous life can be if a male lets himself by tempted by an immoral woman.

This isn't the way we usually look at the problem of immoral sex. More often we think more of Solomon's father, David, and his problem. His activity with Bathsheba was clearly immoral, and he apparently was not seduced by her. His sin was of his own making.

There is clearly another side to this coin, however, and Solomon is making sure we see it.

Solomon was telling his son something that we men know all too well and our sons learn soon enough. Girls and women are appealing, and unless we know what to watch out for, we can be taken in by the wiles of an immoral female.

Of course, in this passage Solomon is spelling out the seductive ways of an adulteress — a woman who knows what she is doing. This is a seasoned veteran who woos men with her sexual allurements. Her lips drip honey and she's a smooth talker. She's trouble with a capital "T."

And Solomon knows that if he doesn't train his son to watch out for this woman at work, she'll snare him quicker than he can say, "But I'm already married." That's why he tells his son to avoid even getting near her. His life, Solomon warns his boy, will come to bitter ruin if he so much as gives her the time of day.

If nothing else, this passage is a clear reminder to us, in a day of increasing infidelity, that adultery is absolutely, undeniably wrong. It should serve as a reminder to each married man who loves God and desires to serve Him that this sin is to be more avoided than a Randy Johnson fastball at your head.

Solomon's calls to "drink water from your own cistern" and to "rejoice in the wife of your youth" are calls for married men of God to rededicate themselves to marital harmony and sexual purity.

But there's another lesson that both dads and sons can learn here. And it has to do with the seductive power of females. The images are graphically clear, suggesting that women have a power over men that can be almost inescapable. Solomon's mention of honey lips and oil-smooth speech, plus his later reference to being captivated, all remind us men that females can put a spell on us that is hard to resist.

And we need to teach our sons how to react to those captivating messages the girls and women send — whether they know they are sending them or not.

This is why it is so important that dads and their sons openly discuss sexual matters — in the right context. Dads can help temper the onslaught of wrong messages that their sons will see and hear in regard to females.

For instance, peer talk about girls will often turn to discussions of female anatomy, and they won't be talking about straight teeth. If a young man has not been instructed by his dad what is appropriate and inappropriate talk about girls, he could, with the "help" of his friends, begin to view girls as nothing but sex objects. Without proper instruction, a boy can easily begin to gravitate toward the girls who make it a point to be sexy, rather than the girls who have a proper view of their sexuality.

Another dangerous ground for a boy who has not been instructed properly by his dad is in media representations of women. Sex sells big time, and a boy who is left to his own imagination will make all kinds of wrong assumptions about women if he is allowed to watch sexy commercials and sex-filled cinema and TV productions without a father's guidance. Those smiling, well-endowed, ready-for-action females who seem to be all over advertisements, network TV screens, and movies may look sweet in their touched-up beauty, but in a sense they are as dangerous as the woman in Proverbs 5. A boy needs a dad to help him develop discernment about both real women and the make-believe women in the media.

If you ever wondered if it is proper and right to have father-son talks about sex, then reread Proverbs. It's not just in Proverbs

5 that Solomon sits down with his son and has a heart-to-heart. He brings up the subject again in chapters 7 and 9.

We men are so easily seduced by women with charm. We must teach our sons to fight off the temptation to be taken in by them. We must instill in them over and over that, once they get married, God wants them to be one-woman men — both physically and mentally.

When it comes to our sons and women, we can do no better than to urge them to heed Solomon's call to "pay attention to my wisdom."

MOTTO

Instruction about sexual matters now can avoid destructive sexual problems later.

DEBRIEFING

1. What have I done to instruct my son about girls and women?

2. In what ways do I try to set the right example for my son by the way I view women, including his mother?

3. Is our family guilty of bringing wrong representations about women into our home through the media?

CALL TO ACTION

1. Depending on the age of my son, within the next month, I will do one of the following things:

   a. Purchase a book that helps me talk to him about sexual matters.

   b. Reread pages 235-249 of *Point Man* for additional help.

   c. Make five instructive comments about male-female relationships.

2. I will stop sexually alluring or seductive images from coming into our house through TV and videos.

3. Without being syrupy or fake, I will demonstrate more clearly to my family that my wife is the object of my attention.

Dear Lord, please help me to have the courage to instruct my son properly in his relationship with females. Thank you for my wife. Help me to cherish her. Guide our family to keep out any improper images or wrong perspectives about sexuality.

LET'S BE FRANK

"How beautiful your sandaled feet, O prince's daughter!" (Song of Solomon 7:1).

MARCHING ORDERS

FROM POINT MAN
Read: Chapter Ten,
pages 235-249

FROM THE BIBLE
Read: Song of
Solomon 7

In today's brief Bible reading, don't miss these points:

• The woman described in this passage is beautiful, and the writer pays tribute to her beauty with clear descriptions.

• There is a sincere appreciation for the woman's beauty, and a desire to spend time with her.

• This picture of devoted love one for another is worth emulating.

THINKING IT THROUGH

Song of Solomon 7 doesn't seem to be a "guy thing."

How many times have you walked up to your wife and said, "Honey, I was just noticing: Your graceful legs are like jewels."

And I'd venture a wild guess that if you snuggled up to her tonight on the living room sofa and whispered, "Your breasts are like two fawns, twins of a gazelle," she'd club you a good one.

And you may have to sleep in the garage if you were to sidle up to her in the kitchen while she's whipping up some cookies and say, "Your nose is like the tower of Lebanon looking toward Damascus." As a bonus, you'd probably get a bowl of flour, sugar, and eggs dumped on your head for that one.

No, guys are more given to two-word descriptions: "Nice legs!"

But for some reason — and those reasons even have Bible scholars scratching their collective heads — this inspired book of the Bible contains descriptions and words that aren't found anywhere else in the Bible. In fact, they don't seem biblical at all.

We often think of the Bible as a genteel book — a book that takes care to be conservative in its presentations. But it contains some very frank passages, and Song of Solomon is one of them.

If the Word of God can be this frank about a male-female relationship in its God-breathed presentation, then surely it helps set a precedent for dads who are seeking to know how to talk to their children about sex.

Look at other passages of Scripture that address the subject of sex, and you'll see that the Bible does not mince words. There is a surprisingly straightforward approach to some things we would rather not talk about.

"Anyone who has sexual relations with an animal must be put to death" (Exodus 22:19). Just the idea of it gives new meaning to the word disgusting, yet the Scripture is clear in its teaching on this subject.

"Do not have sexual relations with your father's wife" (Leviticus 18:8). If a dad ever thought he might be stating the obvious with straight talk about the error of sexual immorality, notice how Scripture deals with this obvious wrong. And this theme continues throughout Leviticus 18.

"It is actually reported that there is sexual immorality among you, and of a kind that does not occur even among pagans: A man has his father's wife" (1 Corinthians 5:1). Imagine the hush that fell over the crowd when this part of Paul's letter was read! It was a real problem, and it had to be dealt with — not swept under a Persian rug.

"The body is not meant for sexual immorality..." (1 Corinthians 6:13). What a great opening line for a father-son talk. It's all right out in the open: Sexual immorality is bad for you. The Bible says so.

"The acts of the sinful nature are obvious: sexual immorality..." (Galatians 5:19). No double-talk, no beating around the bush. Just clear, simple, open talk about sex.

"Marriage should be honored by all, and the marriage bed kept pure, for God will judge the adulterer and all the sexually immoral" (Hebrews 13:4). This is marriage. It is not to be violated. Any questions? Once more, the Bible gives us unmistakable guidelines in unmistakable language.

The pattern is clear. The Bible never uses sexual language in a gratuitous way — never for titillation or entertainment. It is there to make a point, even in the Song of Solomon.

Also, the Bible is abundantly clear in its presentation of sex as an in-marriage-only kind of thing.

These factors can help a dad who is struggling with the best possible way to talk sex with his children:

•The way the Bible presents the topic in a straightforward way indicates it is okay for Dad to be straightforward in a sex-talk presentation.

•The clarity of Scripture in its moral means Dad can be very adamant about morality.

•The way the subject is treated in the Song of Solomon encourages Dad to realize that although sexuality has been dragged through the streets of America and made to look like the activity of slimy people, it is pure and good in the right context.

From the Garden of Eden to Proverbs to Song of Solomon to the Epistles, the Bible honors right sexuality and condemns immoral sex. To a dad who feels overwhelmed with the responsibility of teaching sex in a sex-saturated world, the backing of Scripture is his most valuable tool.

It helps him know that he can pray for God's help, for he is doing God's bidding. Like Solomon, he is dispensing wisdom about a difficult subject, and if he follows God's guidelines, he can be assured of divine help.

When tackling a touchy subject, who can ask for anything more?

MOTTO

A dad who doesn't discuss sex sends his children to the wrong sources.

DEBRIEFING

1. What bothers me the most about discussing this subject with my children?

2. Have I tried to make it an ongoing discussion rather than a one-time lecture?

3. What evidences have I already seen that I need to make more of an effort in this regard?

4. Do I have a complete understanding of the biblical view of sexuality?

CALL TO ACTION

1. If I need further resources, this week I'll visit a Christian bookstore for help.

2. As *Point Man* says on page 248, I'm going to "Go For It" this week by taking the following steps:

a. _____

b. _____

c. _____

Dear heavenly Father, thank you for the beautiful gift of sex. Please help me to use it only the way you designed it. And help me to understand your Word and your teaching on the subject so I can successfully teach it to my children. Guide my words. And prepare their hearts.

Building On The Rock

"The Lord is my rock, my fortress, and my deliverer; my God is my rock, in whom I take refuge. He is my shield and the horn of my salvation, my stronghold" (Psalm 18:2).

MARCHING ORDERS

FROM POINT MAN
Read: Chapter Eleven, pages 252-258

FROM THE BIBLE
Read: Matthew 16:13–20

Don't miss the significance of today's Scripture reading:

• God knows that we need shelter, deliverance, solid ground, protection, salvation, and safety. He provides them all.

• Many people were confused about who Jesus was, but Peter recognized Jesus as the Son of God.

• Jesus called himself a rock that hell itself couldn't budge.

THINKING IT THROUGH

Being a dad in today's world is tough work. It is a job that takes extra energy and special skills. It is a life that must be grounded on something firm and unshakable.

Many dads attempt to build a foundation on money. They become successful in their profession, and they base their worth on the size of their bank account. They stake their ego on their status in the business community. They plan their future around their financial portfolio. What do their children learn from that?

Other dads construct a foundation out of reputation. They carefully build an image that earns respect within the community. They go to the right places, drive the right cars, talk to the right people. What do their children learn from that?

Some dads use their occupation as a foundation. They wrap themselves up in their work, seeking satisfaction. They choose a profession that is respected, and they realize that they are doing important work. They are not happy unless they are either at work or at home thinking about work. What do their children learn from that?

Foundations. There are others that men build their lives on.

But there is only one foundation that will always hold. There is only one building material that will allow a father to build successfully at work, at home, in the community, and for eternity. There is but one foundation that will support him and his family, that will never let his children fail.

That rock is Jesus.

Resting on that rock is so encouraging.

By building on the solid rock, we know we always have a safe place to rest in a world of shifting sands.

Look at what the rock offers, as described in Psalm 18.

•*A fortress.* Like a castle, God provides us protection against both the attacks of Satan and the troubles of life. When troubles do strike, they move us toward God and His protection, turning a bad situation into a positive result. Remember the words of Martin Luther's great song: "A mighty fortress is our God, a bulwark never failing." A dad needs a place like that.

•*A deliverer.* Think of what God delivers us from — from the condemnation of our sin, from the rudderless life we would live without His guidance, from wasting our days on futile activities. And keep this in mind: one day He will deliver us to the glories of heaven.

•*A refuge.* Jesus himself needed an occasional refuge. He went to the mountain top to pray. He visited with Mary and Martha at

Bethany. He went to the Garden in his hour of deepest need. Just as Jesus continually prayed to God, so we have the resource of retreat into His presence.

•*A shield.* We go to the fortress when the war gets extremely fierce, but we can't live in the fortress. We have to go out into the battle. And when we do, we need protection. God is our shield and provides the shield of faith (Ephesians 6:16), equipping us to repel all of the attacks that come along to cast doubt on our faith.

•*A horn of salvation.* Greatest of all, God has provided salvation through faith in Jesus Christ. Without that, we have no foundation, no hope, no reason to concern ourselves with godly living.

•*A stronghold.* In any battle, the army needs a stronghold — a place that has been fortified against the enemy. A place that will not be overrun and destroyed. A retreat. Jesus has all the resources, all the power, all the protection that we ever need. He is the stronghold of our life.

To be the point man in our families, we need to have both feet firmly planted on the rock, Christ Jesus.

Not one foot on the rock and one on our material possessions. Not one foot on the rock and the other on our occupation or profession. Not even one foot on the rock and the other on our family.

How can we tell if that is what we are doing? Perhaps it would help to answer some questions.

Where do we go with problems? To the Lord?

Where do we go for advice? To the Word and Christian leaders?

What do we spend time doing? Worshipping and studying the Word?

What has our passion? Jesus Christ and his church?

What encourages me when I'm down? Prayer and my faith?

We all have other answers that we sometimes put at the end

of those questions. Until we get our glorified bodies and enjoy living in God's presence in heaven, we will continually battle the tendency to get off the rock and make up our own foundations. But if we decide in our hearts to depend on the Lord, we'll find ourselves increasingly looking for the rock to stand up on. Like all of the Christian life, it's a process that will eventually make us much stronger.

No one on earth can come up with a better foundation than the one we have in Jesus Christ. Let's worship and praise him for providing such a gift, and let's honor him by making sure we are solidly on the rock.

Standing on the rock doesn't make being a good father easy, but it makes it possible!

MOTTO

When a dad stands on the rock, Jesus Christ,
he's better able to fulfill his role.

DEBRIEFING

1. When have I stood on the rock and been protected?

2. When have I stepped off the rock and found myself floundering?

3. Which of the characteristics of the Lord as a rock do I most need right now?

CALL TO ACTION

1. I can handle these three situations only if I'm on the rock:

    a. _____

    b. _____

    c. _____

2. I will help my children by sharing with them the rock traits found in Psalm 18:2. I'll set aside time in the next few days to go over it with them.

I love you, O Lord, my strength. Thank you for being my rock and my salvation. Thank you, Jesus, for being a rock that hell itself can't overthrow. Help me to keep standing on the foundation you have built in my life. Help my children to be on the rock.

HOW TO BE WORTH FOLLOWING

"Follow my example, as I follow the example of Christ" (1 Corinthians 11:1).

MARCHING ORDERS

FROM POINT MAN
**Read: Appendix,
pages 259-264**

FROM THE BIBLE
**Read: I Corinthians
10:31–11:1**

As you read today's Scripture passage, consider this:

• Paul's credo was simple: Everything has to be done for Christ's glory.

• It was important to Paul that everyone be treated fairly and unselfishly, because he wanted everyone who came in contact with him to be impressed with Jesus Christ.

• Only if Paul was following Christ should anyone follow him.

THINKING IT THROUGH

Think of all the people your son can be like.

He can be like Mike — the man with the million-dollar jump shot and more moves than a bucket of snakes. Or any number of other sports stars whose exploits your son follows.

He can be like Michael — the man with the moon walk and the million-selling records and tapes. Or any number of music personalities.

He can be like Steve Largent — the athlete-turned politician who is in Washington because he says he thinks he can help. Or any number of political figures.

Or he can be like you.

Most probably, he will be.

He sees you every day as you interact with him and the rest of the family.

He sees you at church serving God.

He hears you on the phone talking with friends, colleagues, and others.

He sees you at his ball games and hears how you respond to his mistakes and to bad officiating.

He sees you handle money problems, discipline problems, husband-wife squabbles, neighbor conflicts, driving challenges, and hundreds of other incidents where you show what you are really made of.

Yes, more than anyone else, your son will end up being like you.

The key question, then, is this: How can we tell if we are being the kind of person our sons should follow?

The answer is found in Paul's wise words to the people at the church in Corinth. He told them this: "Follow my example, as I follow the example of Christ."

If we are following Jesus Christ with our walk and with our talk, then our kids can follow us. If we are not following Jesus Christ, we'd better hope our children don't emulate us.

To be the best point man we can be, we must follow the ultimate point man: Jesus Christ.

Let's look at Jesus' life from four perspectives as a checklist for our own lives. After seeing how he handled some situations, we can test ourselves to see if we are doing what he would do in similar circumstances.

•*How Jesus handled his emotions.* We can't overlook the fact that Jesus, the true God-man, had human characteristics. If we forget that, then we won't see him as a viable example. Jesus cried, was displeased, and expressed agony.

He also grew angry. In Mark 11, we can read about his anger at the dishonest people in the temple at Jerusalem. Jesus was upset enough to overthrow the moneychangers' tables and kick them out of God's house. Notice, though, that Jesus did not act impulsively. He drove out the bad guys on his second visit to the temple, not his first. Also, Jesus was not reacting to a personal affront. He was angry because the people were disobeying God and defiling the temple. And Jesus was under control. He turned over tables but did not harm the animals and birds (see John 2:13–16).

When we are angry, do we show restraint, do we avoid reacting to personal affronts, and do we reserve our anger for immorality?

Another emotion Jesus showed was compassion. After Jesus heard that John the Baptist had been killed, he went away to be alone (Matthew 14:10–21). Soon, however, he was discovered by the people clamoring to see him. When the people came to him, "He was moved with compassion for them, and healed their sick" (Matthew 14:14).

Do we show compassion for others despite our own difficulties? This is such an important trait for dads, for we always carry burdens with us, yet we must stop and have compassion and care for our family and others.

•*How Jesus treated others.* We cannot escape something Jesus said about getting along with other people. He told us that the second great commandment is to love our neighbors as ourselves. The bottom line for how Jesus treated others is love.

For instance, look at how he treated the down and out. Jesus got into all kinds of trouble for his willingness to show love for society's outcasts. He paid special attention to a leper, despite the social rules against doing so (Mark 1:40–45). He also spent so much time working with "bad" people he was derisively called "a friend of sinners."

And notice how he treated his friends. He served them. Here was the King of the universe, yet he did servants' tasks for the disciples. He helped them fish. He fixed them breakfast. He washed their feet.

Our children notice how we respond to the needy people of this world — the down and out. What do they hear us saying about people who haven't the blessings we enjoy? What do they see us do to help them?

And when they see us interact with our friends, do they see someone who is willing to give to make the relationship work?

• *How Jesus walked with God.* Two of the most important examples Jesus set for us are his examples of prayer and the use of Scripture. Over and over we see Jesus praying, both in public and private. In fact, he taught the disciples how to pray, and isn't that a great lesson we should be teaching our children? And Jesus used the Scriptures several times during his earthly life, again setting the example for us. He used it to correct error (he referred to both Isaiah 56:7 and Jeremiah 7:11 when he cleansed the temple of moneychangers). He used Scripture to teach (see Luke 10:25–28). He used Scripture to repel the temptations of Satan (Matthew 4:1–11).

Our walk with God in many ways is connected to those two disciplines: prayer and Scripture study. Our example to our children will be evident to them if they see us practicing them both.

Jesus, it is true, is a tough act to follow. But he wasn't acting. He was genuinely living as a person should live on this earth. When he left to return to heaven, he left behind a helper, the Holy Spirit. With his help, we can grow more and more like Jesus every day.

As we do, we'll be better and better examples for our children.

And isn't that what being a point man is all about?

*The more we live like Jesus, the more our children
can trust our example.*

DEBRIEFING

1. Would anyone mistake me for a disciple of Jesus? What characteristics do I share with the Lord?

2. When would my children say I am most like Jesus? When would they say I am least like him?

3. What characteristic of Jesus do I most admire?

CALL TO ACTION

1. This motto will be prominently displayed on my car dashboard, my office wall, or my TV: "What Would Jesus Do?"

2. This week, I will work on these two traits of Jesus:

    a. _____

    b. _____

3. I will try to eliminate these two negative personal traits:

    a. _____

    b. _____

4. I will ask my son what kind of example he thinks I've been for him, and see if he has any suggestions for times when I have not been like Jesus.

Dear Father, thank you for Jesus' example. Thank you for recording in your Word some of his day-to-day experiences for our benefit. Please help me each day to become more like the Savior in the way I handle things. Show me my error and correct my ways.